everyday Phonics

Intervention A

Table of Contents

Using Everyday Phonics Intervention Activities

Current research identifies phonemic awareness and phonics as the essential skills for reading success.

- **Phonemic awareness** is the ability to notice, think about, and work with the individual sounds in spoken words. Before children learn to read print, they need to become aware of how the sounds in words work. They must understand that words are made up of speech sounds, or phonemes.

- **Phonics** instruction teaches children the relationships between the letters (graphemes) of written language and the individual sounds (phonemes) of spoken language. Children learn to use the relationships to read and write words. Knowing the relationships will help children recognize familiar words accurately and automatically, and "decode" new words.

Although some students master these skills easily during regular classroom instruction, many others need additional re-teaching opportunities to master these essential skills. The Everyday Phonics Intervention Activities series provides easy-to-use, five-day intervention units for Grades K–5. These units are structured around a research-based Model-Guide-Practice-Apply approach. You can use these activities in a variety of intervention models, including Response to Intervention (RTI).

Getting Started

In just five simple steps, Everyday Phonics Intervention Activities provides everything you need to identify students' phonetic needs and to provide targeted intervention.

1. PRE-ASSESS to identify students' Phonemic Awareness and Phonics needs.

Use the pre-assessment on the CD-ROM to identify the skills your students need to master.

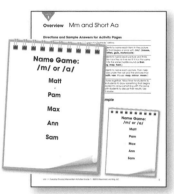

Day 1

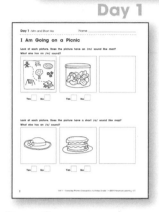

2. MODEL the skill.

Every five-day unit targets a specific phonetic element. On Day 1, use the teacher prompts and reproducible activity page to introduce and model the skill.

Day 2

Day 3

Day 4

3. GUIDE PRACTICE and APPLY.

Use the reproducible practice activities for Days 2, 3, and 4 to build students' understanding and skill-proficiency.

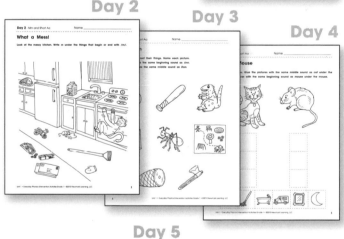

Day 5

4. MONITOR progress.

Administer the Day 5 reproducible assessment to monitor each student's progress and to make instructional decisions.

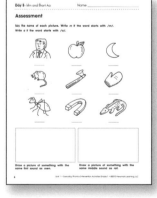

5. POST-ASSESS to document student progress.

Use the post-assessment on the CD-ROM to measure students' progress as a result of your interventions.

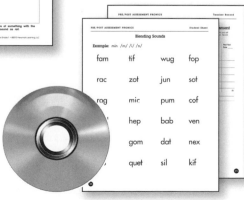

Standards-Based Phonemic Awareness & Phonics Skills in Everyday Intervention Activities

The Phonemic Awareness and Phonics skills found in the Everyday Intervention Activities series are introduced developmentally and spiral from one grade to the next. The chart below shows the skill areas addressed at each grade level in this series.

Everyday Phonics Intervention Activities Series Skills	K	1	2	3	4	5
Phonemic Awareness	✔	✔	✔	✔		
Letter Identificaton and Formation	✔	✔				
Sound/Symbol Relationships	✔	✔				
Short Vowels		✔				
Consonants		✔				
Long Vowels			✔	✔		
Blends			✔	✔		
Digraphs			✔	✔		
Variant Vowels			✔	✔		
CVCe Syllable Patterns			✔	✔	✔	✔
Closed Syllable Patterns				✔	✔	✔
Open Syllable Patterns				✔	✔	✔
r-Controlled Syllable Patterns				✔	✔	✔
Diphthongs				✔	✔	✔
Silent Letters				✔	✔	✔
Contractions				✔	✔	✔
Regular and Irregular Plurals				✔	✔	✔
Prefixes					✔	✔
Compound Words					✔	✔
Comparatives						✔
Greek and Latin Roots						✔
Homographs and Homophones						✔
Word Origins						✔

Everyday Phonics Intervention Activities Grade 1 • ©2010 Newmark Learning, LLC

Using Everyday Intervention for RTI

According to the National Center on Response to Intervention, RTI "integrates assessment and intervention within a multi-level prevention system to maximize student achievement and to reduce behavior problems." This model of instruction and assessment allows schools to identify at-risk students, monitor their progress, provide research-proven interventions, and "adjust the intensity and nature of those interventions depending on a student's responsiveness."

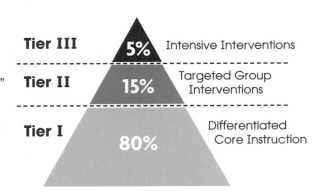

RTI models vary from district to district, but the most prevalent model is a three-tiered approach to instruction and assessment.

The Three Tiers of RTI	Using Everyday Intervention Activities
Tier I: Differentiated Core Instruction • Designed for all students • Preventive, proactive, standards-aligned instruction • Whole- and small-group differentiated instruction • Ninety-minute, daily core reading instruction in the five essential skill areas: phonics, phonemic awareness, comprehension, vocabulary, fluency	• Use whole-group comprehension mini-lessons to introduce and guide practice with comprehension strategies that all students need to learn. • Use any or all of the units in the order that supports your core instructional program.
Tier II: Targeted Group Interventions • For at-risk students • Provide thirty minutes of daily instruction beyond the ninety-minute Tier I core reading instruction • Instruction is conducted in small groups of three to five students with similar needs	• Select units based on your students' areas of need (the pre-assessment can help you identify these). • Use the units as week-long, small-group mini-lessons.
Tier III: Intensive Interventions • For high-risk students experiencing considerable difficulty in reading • Provide up to sixty minutes of additional intensive intervention each day in addition to the ninety-minute Tier I core reading instruction • More intense and explicit instruction • Instruction conducted individually or with smaller groups of one to three students with similar needs	• Select units based on your students' areas of need. • Use the units as one component of an intensive comprehension intervention program.

Overview   Mm and Short Aa

Directions and Sample Answers for Activity Pages

Day 1	See "Model the Skill" below.
Day 2	Read the title and directions aloud. Invite students to name each item in the picture. Then help students write **m** under each picture that begins or ends with **/m/**. (**mouse, milk, ham, monkey, broom, mail, money, mitten, gum, motorcycle**)
Day 3	Read the title and directions aloud. Invite students to name each picture and think about where they hear **/a/**. Then help students color the picture red if it has the same beginning sound as **Ann** and color it blue if it has the same middle sound as **Dan**. (Red: **apple, alligator, ant, ax**. Blue: **bat, bag, map, ham**.)
Day 4	Read the title and directions aloud. Invite students to name each picture. Then help students glue the pictures with **/a/** in the middle under the cat and the pictures that start with **/m/** under the mouse. (Cat: **pan, bath, van**. Mouse: **mop, mirror, moon**.)
Day 5	Read the directions aloud and name the pictures together. Allow time for students to complete the first task. Then say **men** and ask students to draw something that begins with the same sound. Next, say **rat** and ask student to draw something with the same middle sound. Afterward, meet individually with students to discuss their results. Use their responses to plan further instruction and review.

Model the Skill

◆ Hand out the Day 1 activity page.

◆ **Say:** *Imagine we are going on a picnic. First, we'll pack things that begin with **/m/**. Can we pack a map?* Allow time for students to say the word with you and mark **Yes**. Repeat with **nuts**. Then invite students to draw one more thing they could pack that begins with **/m/**.

◆ **Say:** *Now we will pack things with **/a/** in the middle. Can we pack a hat?* Allow time for students to say the word with you and mark **Yes**. Repeat with **cake**. Then invite students to draw one more thing they could pack with **/a/** in the middle.

◆ Say a student's name in the class, or the school, that begins or ends with **/m/** or has **/a/** in it. Write the name on chart paper. Then invite students to suggest other names.

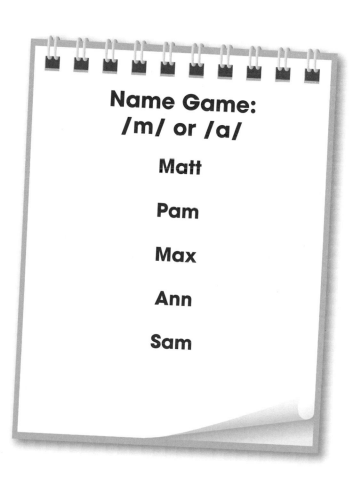

Name Game:
/m/ or /a/

Matt

Pam

Max

Ann

Sam

I Am Going on a Picnic

Look at each picture. Does the picture have an /m/ sound like man?
What else has an /m/ sound?

Yes ☐ **No** ☐   **Yes** ☐ **No** ☐

Look at each picture. Does the picture have a short /a/ sound like map?
What else has an /a/ sound?

Yes ☐ **No** ☐   **Yes** ☐ **No** ☐

          Unit 1 • Everyday Phonics Intervention Activities Grade 1 • ©2010 Newmark Learning, LLC

Name _____

What a Mess!

Look at the messy kitchen. Write *m* under the things that begin or end with /m/.

Ann or Dan

Help Ann and Dan sort their things. Name each picture. Color it red if it has the same beginning sound as *Ann*. Color it blue if it has the same middle sound as *Dan*.

Cat and Mouse

Cut out the pictures. Glue the pictures with the same middle sound as *cat* under the cat. Glue the pictures with the same beginning sound as *mouse* under the mouse.

Assessment

Say the name of each picture. Write **m** if the word starts with **/m/**. Write **a** if the word starts with **/a/**.

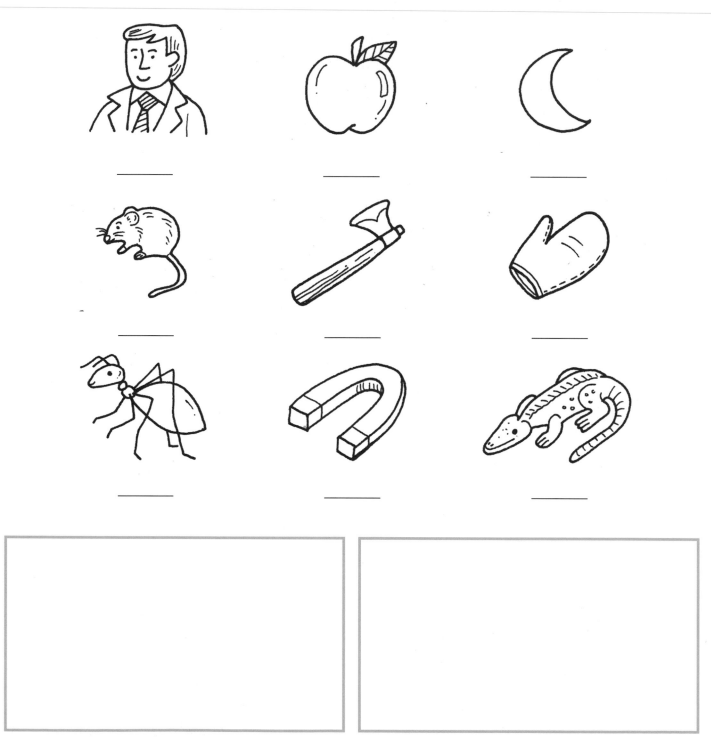

Draw a picture of something with the same first sound as **men**.

Draw a picture of something with the same middle sound as **rat**.

  Unit 1 • Everyday Phonics Intervention Activities Grade 1 • ©2010 Newmark Learning, LLC

Overview   Ss

Directions and Sample Answers for Activity Pages

Day 1	See "Model the Skill" below.
Day 2	Read the title and directions aloud. Invite students to name each picture. Then help students write **s** under each picture that begins with **/s/**. (**sock, sandwich, sun, saw, six**)
Day 3	Read the title and directions aloud. Invite students to name each picture. Then help students glue the pictures that begin with **/s/** on the sun and the pictures that end with **/s/** on the bus. (Sun: **saddle, seven, soap**. Bus: **grass, dress, gas**.)
Day 4	Read the title and directions aloud. Help students write Sam's name on his T-shirt. Then help them cut out the letters and glue them on the lines to make a sentence about Sam. (I am Sam.)
Day 5	Read the directions aloud and name the pictures together. Allow time for students to complete the first task. Then pronounce the words **am** and **Sam** and ask students to write them on the lines. Afterward, meet individually with students to discuss their results. Use their responses to plan further instruction and review.

Model the Skill

◆ Hand out the Day 1 activity page and some crayons.

◆ **Say:** *I will pretend I am going to the sea. I can only bring things that begin with /s/. Can I bring sandals or boots? Color the one that starts with /s/.* Allow time for students to color the sandals.

◆ **Ask:** *Can I bring a sandwich or pizza? Color the lunch that begins with /s/.* Allow time for students to color the sandwich.

◆ **Ask:** *Can I bring a sailboat or a pail? Color the toy that begins with /s/.* Allow time for students to color the sailboat. Then ask them to draw one more item they can bring that begins with **/s/**. Invite them to share their drawings with the group.

◆ Point out objects you can see in the classroom that start with **/s/**. Write a few on chart paper and read the words aloud. Then invite students to add to the list.

Sound Search: /s/

scissors

soap

socks

sign

sack

songbook

sight words

safety poster

At the Sea

Color the things that start with /s/ like sea.

Then draw something else that starts with /s/.

Searching for Sue

Help Sal Salamander find his sister Sue.

Write s under each picture that begins with /s/.

S Sort

Cut out the pictures. Glue the pictures that begin with **/s/** on the sun.
Glue the pictures that end with **/s/** on the bus.

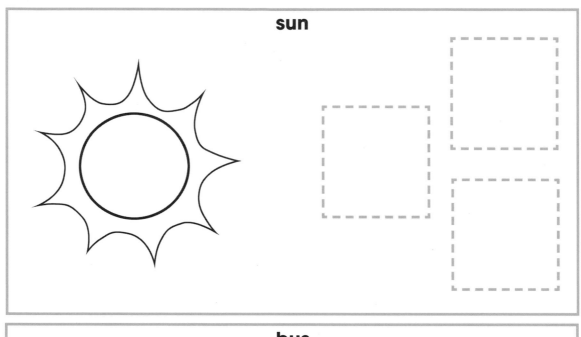

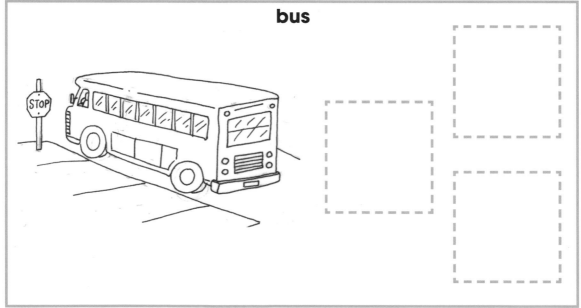

Unit 2 • *Everyday Phonics Intervention Activities Grade 1* • ©2010 Newmark Learning, LLC

A Boy Named Sam

This boy is Sam. Write *Sam* on the boy's T-shirt.

Cut out the letters. Glue the letters on the lines to make a sentence about Sam. Then read your sentence to a friend.

Name _____

Assessment

Say the name of each picture. Write **s** if the word starts with **/s/**.

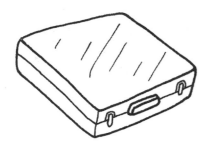

_____   _____   _____

_____   _____   _____

_____   _____   _____

Listen to your teacher say each word. Write the words on the lines.

1. _____

2. _____

   Unit 2 • Everyday Phonics Intervention Activities Grade 1 • ©2010 Newmark Learning, LLC

Overview   Tt

Directions and Sample Answers for Activity Pages

Day 1	See "Model the Skill" below.
Day 2	Read aloud the title and directions. Invite students to name each picture. Then help students write X on each picture that begins with **/t/** and O on each picture that ends with **/t/**. (X: **toothbrush, table, tongue, turtle, tape**. O: **pot, bat, cat, foot**.)
Day 3	Read aloud the title and directions. Invite students to name each picture. Then help students glue the pictures that begin with **/t/** under the tortoise and the pictures that end with **/t/** under the rabbit. (Tortoise: **tooth, tea, tomato, top**. Rabbit: **ant, carrot**.)
Day 4	Read aloud the title and directions. Help students cut out the letters and glue them on the lines to spell each word. (**mat, sat**)
Day 5	Read the directions aloud and name the pictures together. Allow time for students to complete the first task. Then pronounce the words **sat** and **Sam** and ask students to write them on the lines. Afterward, meet individually with students to discuss their results. Use their responses to plan further instruction and review.

Model the Skill

◆ Hand out the Day 1 activity page and some crayons.

◆ **Say:** *Let's pretend we are on a road trip. When we see something that begins with /t/, let's color it red. Does **tire** begin with /t/?* Allow time for students to say the word with you and color it red. Repeat with **turtle** and **toll**. Then invite students to draw one more thing that begins with **/t/**.

◆ **Say:** *Now let's look for things that end with /t/ and color them blue. Does boat end with /t/?* Allow time for students to say the word with you and color it blue. Repeat with **hat** and **boot**. Then invite students to draw one more thing that ends with **/t/**.

◆ Point out objects you can see in the classroom that start with **/t/**. Write a few on chart paper and read the words aloud. Then invite students to add to the list.

Sound Search: /t/

tape

table

teacher

tissue

tile

telephone

ten

Name _____

On the Road

Circle the things that have a /t/ sound.

Then draw two other things that have a /t/ sound.

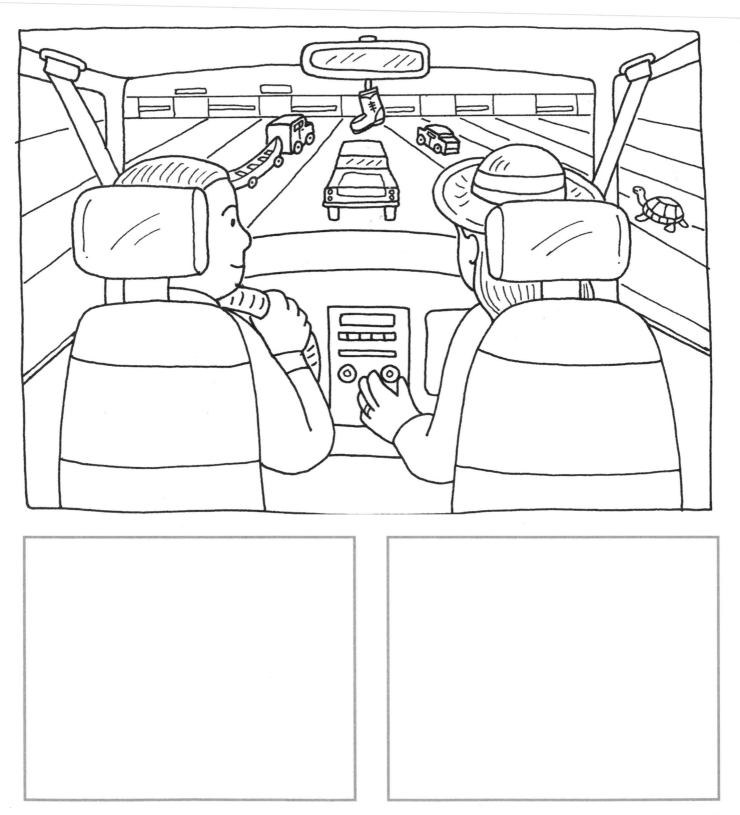

Unit 3 • Everyday Phonics Intervention Activities Grade 1 • ©2010 Newmark Learning, LLC

Tic-Tac-Toe

Write an X on each picture that begins with the same sound as tiger. Write an O on each picture that ends with the same sound as cat. Which animal wins?

Tortoise and Rabbit

Cut out the pictures. Glue the ones with the same beginning sound as *tortoise* under the tortoise. Glue the pictures with the same ending sound as *rabbit* under the rabbit. The animal with more things wins the race!

Unit 3 • Everyday Phonics Intervention Activities Grade 1 • ©2010 Newmark Learning, LLC

Sound It Out

Say the picture word. Listen to the sounds at the beginning, middle, and end.
Cut out the letters and glue them to make or complete the word.

a	m	s	t	t

Assessment

Say the name of each picture. Write *t* if the word starts with /t/.

 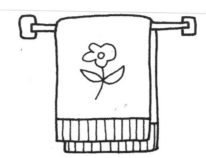 

_____ _____ _____

  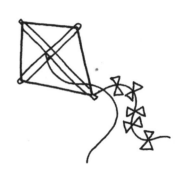

_____ _____ _____

_____ _____ _____

Listen to your teacher say each word. Write the words on the lines.

1. _____

2. _____

 Unit 3 • Everyday Phonics Intervention Activities Grade 1 • ©2010 Newmark Learning, LLC

Overview Nn

Directions and Sample Answers for Activity Pages

Day 1	See "Model the Skill" below.
Day 2	Read aloud the title and directions. Invite students to name each picture. Then help students write **n** under each picture that begins with **/n/**. (**nose, needle, nurse, nine**)
Day 3	Read aloud the title and directions. Invite students to name each picture. Then help students glue the pictures that begin with **/n/** under the bowl of noodles and the pictures that end with **/n/** under the corn. (Noodles: **newspaper**, **nose**, **nurse**. Corn: **horn**, **moon**, **lemon**.)
Day 4	Read aloud the title and directions. Help students cut out the letters and glue them on the lines to spell each word. (**ant, man, mat**)
Day 5	Read the directions aloud and name the pictures together. Allow time for students to complete the first task. Then pronounce the words **man** and **tan** and ask students to write them on the lines. Afterward, meet individually with students to discuss their results. Use their responses to plan further instruction and review.

Model the Skill

◆ Hand out the Day 1 activity page.

◆ **Say:** *There are lots of neat things to see at the circus. When we see something that begins with **/n/**, let's draw a circle around it. Look at the giraffe's neck. Does **neck** begin with **/n/**?* Allow time for students to say the word with you, and draw a circle around it. Repeat with **nut**. Then invite students to draw one more thing that begins with **/n/**.

◆ **Say:** *Now let's look for things that end with **/n/** and draw a square around them. Does **clown** end with **/n/**?* Allow time for students to say the word with you and draw a square around it. Repeat with **bal-loon**. Then invite students to draw one more thing that ends with **/n/**.

◆ Name things we use or do in our everyday lives that begin with **/n/**. Write a few on chart paper and read the words aloud. Then invite students to add to the list.

Sound Search: /n/

napkin

nickel

newspaper

nap

nod

Circus Time!

Circle the things that have an /n/ sound.

Then draw two things that have an /n/ sound.

Ned Goes North

Help Ned travel to the North Pole. Write _n_ under each picture that begins with /n/.

Sort It Out

Cut out the pictures. Glue the pictures that begin with /n/ under the bowl of noodles. Glue the pictures that end with /n/ under the corn.

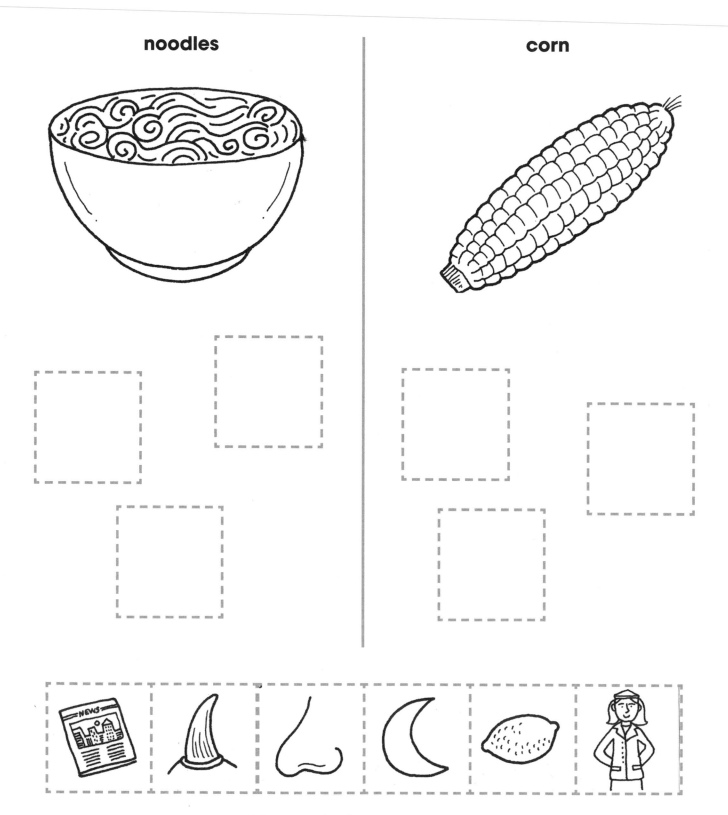

noodles

corn

Sound It Out

Say the picture word. Listen to the sounds at the beginning, middle, and end.
Cut out the letters and glue them to make each word.

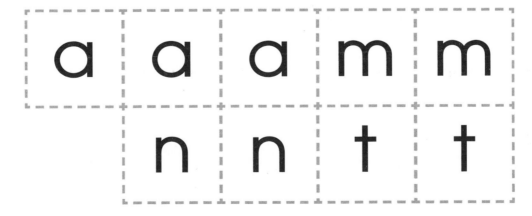

Assessment

Say the name of each picture. Write *n* if the word starts with */n/*.

_____   _____   _____

_____   _____   _____

_____   _____

Listen to your teacher say each word. Write the words on the lines.

1. _____

2. _____

Overview Short Ii

Directions and Sample Answers for Activity Pages

Day 1	See "Model the Skill" below.
Day 2	Read the title and directions aloud. Invite students to name each picture. Help students circle the picture and write the letter **i** if it has the same middle sound as **Finn** and **fish**. (**ring, crib, lips, pin**)
Day 3	Read aloud the title and directions. Invite students to name each picture. Then help students glue pictures with the same middle sound as **Jack** in Jack's basket. Help them glue pictures with the same middle sound as **Jill** in Jill's basket. (Jack: **pants, flag, cat**. Jill: **chick, stick, bib**.)
Day 4	Read aloud the title and directions. Help students cut out the letters and glue them on the lines to spell each word. (**pin, mitt, sit**)
Day 5	Read the directions aloud and name the pictures together. Allow time for students to complete the first task. Then pronounce the words **sit** and **tin** and ask students to write them on the lines. Afterward, meet individually with students to discuss their results. Use their responses to plan further instruction and review.

Model the Skill

◆ Hand out the Day 1 activity page and some crayons.

◆ **Say:** *Kim likes to sing. But Kim only likes to sing about things that have* **/i/** *in the middle. Will Kim sing about a pig or a pug? Color the one with* **/i/** *in the middle.* Allow time for students to color the pig.

◆ **Ask:** *Can Kim sing about a foot or a fish? Color the picture that has the* **/i/** *sound in it.* Allow time for students to color the fish.

◆ **Ask:** *Can Kim sing about a sink or a skunk? Color the one that has* **/i/** *in the middle.* Allow time for students to color the sink. Then ask them to draw one more thing Kim can sing about that has **/i/** in the middle. Invite them to share their drawings with the group.

◆ Name some actions people do that have the **/i/** sound in the middle of the word. Write a few on chart paper and read the words aloud. Then invite students to add to the list.

Sound Search: /i/

wink

think

blink

fix

skip

snip

rip

zip

drink

Name _____

Kim Sings

Color the pictures that have an */i/* sound like *Kim.*

Then draw something that has an */i/* sound.

Unit 5 • Everyday Phonics Intervention Activities Grade 1 • ©2010 Newmark Learning, LLC

Finn the Fish

Help Finn the fish swim across the sea. Circle the pictures with the same middle sound as *Finn* and *fish*, and write the letter *i* on the line below.

Name _____

Jack and Jill

Cut out and name each picture. Glue the ones with the same middle sound as *Jack* in Jack's basket. Glue the pictures with the same middle sound as *Jill* in Jill's basket.

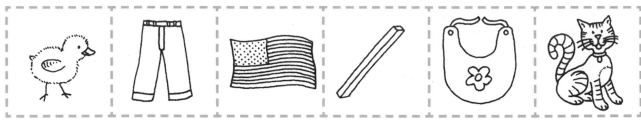

Sound It Out

**Say the picture word. Listen to the sounds at the beginning, middle, and end.
Cut out the letters and glue them to make or complete each word.**

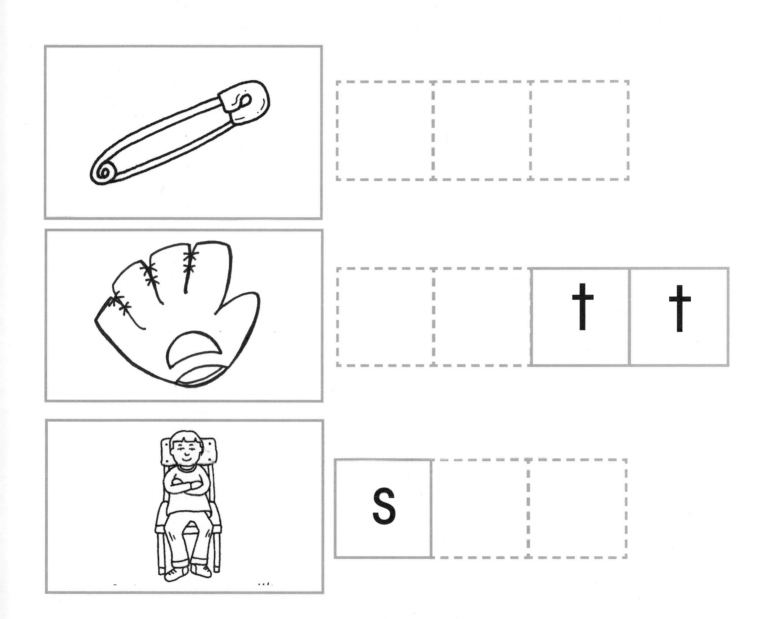

Assessment

Say the name of each picture. Write *i* if the word has /i/ in it.

_____

_____

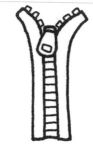

_____

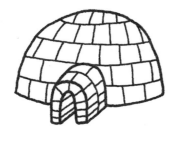

_____

_____

_____

_____

_____

_____

Listen to your teacher say each word. Write the words on the lines.

1. _____

2. _____

Unit 5 • Everyday Phonics Intervention Activities Grade 1 • ©2010 Newmark Learning, LLC

Overview   Ff

Directions and Sample Answers for Activity Pages

Day 1	See "Model the Skill" below.
Day 2	Read aloud the title and directions. Invite students to name each picture. Then help students identify each picture that begins with /f/. (**fairy, flower, fox, fence**)
Day 3	Read aloud the title and directions. Invite students to name each picture. Then help students glue the pictures that begin with /f/ under the fork and the pictures that end with /f/ under knife. (Fork: **feather, football, fish**. Knife: **elf, leaf, wolf**.)
Day 4	Read aloud the title and directions. Help students cut out the letters and glue them on the lines to spell each word. (**fan, fin, fit**)
Day 5	Read the directions aloud and name the pictures together. Allow time for students to complete the first task. Then pronounce the words **fat** and **fan** and ask students to write them on the lines. Afterward, meet individually with students to discuss their results. Use their responses to plan further instruction and review.

Model the Skill

◆ Hand out the Day 1 activity page and some crayons.

◆ **Say:** *Fred went to the Fun Fair on Friday. Everything there began with the same sound as* **fun***! Let's figure out what Fred saw at the fair. Did he see a fish or a tiger? Color the animal that starts with* **/f/***.* Allow time for students to color the fish.

◆ **Ask:** *Did Fred eat a hot dog or French fries? Color the food that begins with* **/f/***.* Allow time for students to color the French fries.

◆ **Ask:** *Did Fred ride the roller coaster or the Ferris wheel? Color the ride that begins with* **/f/***.*

◆ Allow time for students to color the Ferris wheel. Then ask students to draw one more item they might see at the fair that begins with **/f/**. Invite them to share their drawings with the group.

◆ Point out objects you can see in the classroom that start with **/f/**. Write a few on chart paper and read the words aloud. Then invite students to find more to add to the list.

Sound Search: /f/
folder
floor
files
phone
photos
facts
furnace
felt
faces
fish

Fun Fair

Color the things that start with **/f/**. Then draw something else that starts with **/f/**.

Unit 6 • Everyday Phonics Intervention Activities Grade 1 • ©2010 Newmark Learning, LLC

Leap Frog

Help Frog leap across the pond. Draw a circle around pictures that begin with the same sound as *frog*.

Name _____

Fork and Knife

Cut out the pictures and name them. Glue the pictures that begin with **/f/** under the fork. Glue the pictures that end with **/f/** under the knife.

Fork	Knife

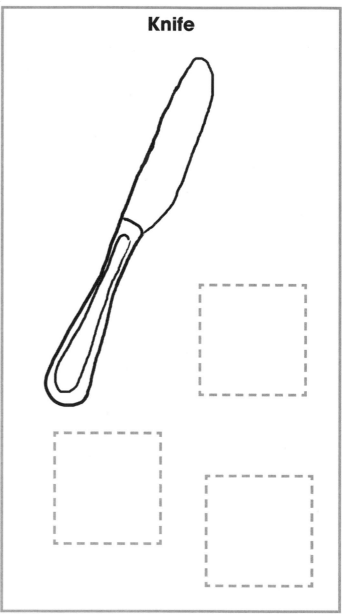

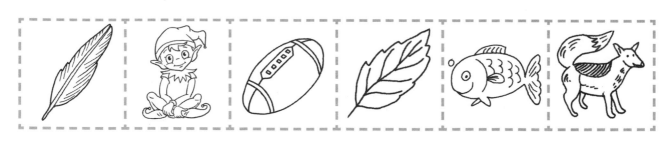

Unit 6 • Everyday Phonics Intervention Activities Grade 1 • ©2010 Newmark Learning, LLC

Sound It Out

Say the picture word. Listen to the sounds at the beginning, middle, and end.
Cut out the letters and glue them to make each word.

Assessment

Say the name of each picture. Write **f** if the word has **/f/** sound in it.

_____   _____   _____

_____   _____   _____

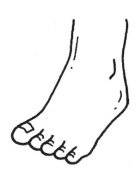

_____   _____   _____

Listen to your teacher say each word. Write the words on the lines.

1. _____

2. _____

Overview Pp

Directions and Sample Answers for Activity Pages

Day 1	See "Model the Skill" below.
Day 2	Read the title and directions aloud. Invite students to name each picture. Then help students write **p** under each picture that begins with **/p/**. (**peach, pear, pumpkin, potato**)
Day 3	Read the title and directions aloud. Invite students to name each picture. Then help students glue the pictures that begin with **/p/** on the pot and the pictures that end with **/p/** on the top. (Pot: **peel, pants, penny.** Top: **cup, rope, trap.**)
Day 4	Read aloud the title and directions. Help students cut out the letters and glue them on the lines to spell each word. (**pan, map, pin**)
Day 5	Read the directions aloud and name the pictures together. Allow time for students to complete the first task. Then pronounce the words **nap** and **pit** and ask students to write them on the lines. Afterward, meet individually with students to discuss their results. Use their responses to plan further instruction and review.

Model the Skill

◆ Hand out the Day 1 activity page.

◆ **Say:** *Pilar is having a party! What will you bring? Pilar loves things that begin with* **/p/**, *like her name, Pilar. When we see something that begins with* **/p/**, *we'll draw a box around it. Does pizza begin with* **/p/**? Allow time for students to say the word with you. Then have them draw a box around it. Repeat with **pig** and **puppet**. Invite students to draw one more thing that begins with **/p/**.

◆ **Say:** *Pilar does not want things that end in* **/p/**. *Let's draw an X through things that end in* **/p/**. *Does* **sheep** *end with* **/p/**? Allow time for students to say the word with you and draw an X through it. Repeat with **jeep** and **mop**.

◆ Name foods that begin with **/p/**. Write a few on chart paper and read the words aloud. Then invite students to add to the list.

Food Game: /p/

plum

pear

pasta

pizza

pancake

pineapple

potato

Name _____

Pilar Is Having a Party

Draw a box around the things that start with /p/.

Draw an X on the things that end with /p/.

Now draw a food that begins with /p/.

P in My Pie

You are baking a pie with items that begin with the same sound as *pie*.
Write *p* under the things that begin with /p/.

Pot Top

Cut out the pictures. Glue the pictures that begin with /p/ on the pot.
Glue the pictures that end with /p/ on the top.

pot

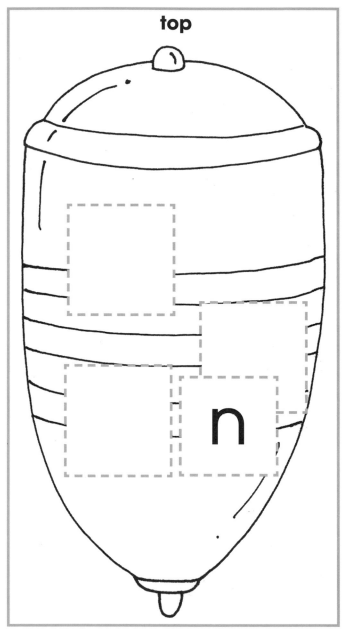

top

n

Unit 7 • Everyday Phonics Intervention Activities Grade 1 • ©2010 Newmark Learning, LLC

Sound It Out

Say the picture word. Listen to the sounds at the beginning, middle, and end.
Cut out the letters and glue them to make each word.

Name _____

Assessment

Say the name of each picture. Write *p* if the word starts with /p/.

_____

_____

_____

_____

_____

_____

_____

_____

_____

Listen to your teacher say each word. Write the words on the lines.

1. _____

2. _____

Unit 7 • Everyday Phonics Intervention Activities Grade 1 • ©2010 Newmark Learning, LLC

Overview   Short Oo

Directions and Sample Answers for Activity Pages

Day 1	See "Model the Skill" below.
Day 2	Read the title and directions aloud. Invite students to name each picture. Help students color the pictures that have the same middle sound as **hop**. (**box, lock, doll, fox, log**)
Day 3	Read aloud the title and directions. Invite students to name each picture. Then help students glue pictures with the same middle sound as **box** in the box. (**pot, frog, rock**)
Day 4	Read aloud the title and directions. Help students cut out the letters and glue them on the lines to spell each word. (**mop, pot, top**)
Day 5	Read the directions aloud and name the pictures together. Allow time for students to complete the first task. Then pronounce the words **pop** and **not** and ask students to write them on the lines. Afterward, meet individually with students to discuss their results. Use their responses to plan further instruction and review.

Model the Skill

◆ Hand out the Day 1 activity page.

◆ **Say:** *Our class is full of things that have the middle sound /o/. Does knob have /o/ in the middle?* Allow time for students to say the word with you and mark **Yes**.

◆ **Ask:** *Does book have /o/ in the middle?* Point out that **book** has the letter **o** in it, but that it is not the same /o/ sound as in **knob**. Allow time for students to repeat the word with you and mark **No**.

◆ Repeat with the rest of the pictures. Then invite students to draw one more classroom item with an /o/ in the middle.

◆ Say a student's name in the class, or the school, that has /o/ in the middle or the beginning. Write the name on chart paper. Then invite students to suggest other names.

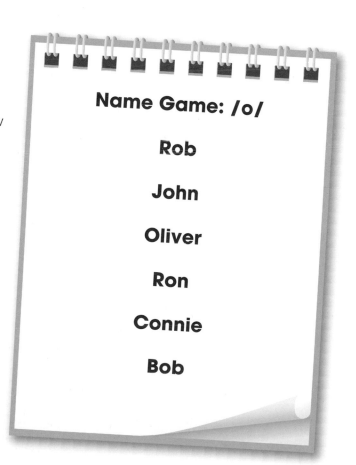

Name Game: /o/

Rob

John

Oliver

Ron

Connie

Bob

Name _____

Sound Search

Look at each picture. Does the picture have an */o/* sound like *pop*?

Yes ☐ No ☐   Yes ☐ No ☐   Yes ☐ No ☐

Yes ☐ No ☐   Yes ☐ No ☐

Now draw something in the classroom with an */o/* in the middle.

_____

Hop to It

Help Polly play hopscotch. Color the pictures that have the same middle sound as *hop*.

Box It

Cut out and name each picture.

Glue the ones with the same middle sound as *box* in the box.

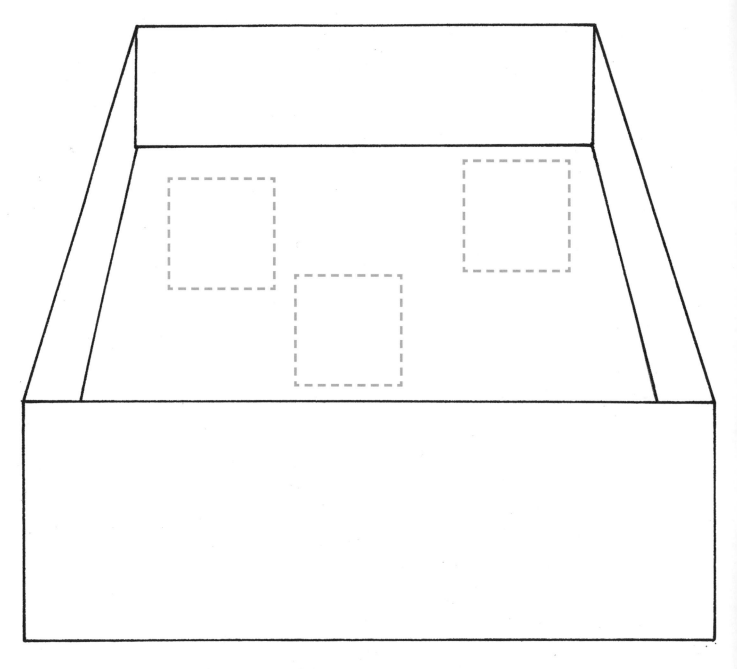

Sound It Out

Say the picture word. Listen to the sounds at the beginning, middle, and end. Cut out the letters and glue them to make each word.

Assessment

Say the name of each picture. Write *o* if the word has /o/ in it.

_____   _____   _____

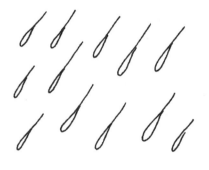

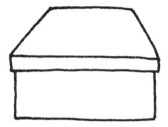

_____   _____   _____

_____   _____   _____

Listen to your teacher say each word. Write the words on the lines.

1. _____

2. _____

Unit 8 • Everyday Phonics Intervention Activities Grade 1 • ©2010 Newmark Learning, LLC

Overview Cc

Directions and Sample Answers for Activity Pages

Day 1	See "Model the Skill" below.
Day 2	Read the title and directions aloud. Invite students to name each picture. Then help students write **c** under each picture that begins with **/k/**. (**cows, corn, cat, cart, cobweb**)
Day 3	Read aloud the title and directions. Invite students to name each picture. Then help students glue the pictures that begin with **/k/** in the cart and the pictures that begin with **/s/** in the sack. (Cart: **comb, coin, cookie**. Sack: **sandwich, sock, sun**.)
Day 4	Read aloud the title and directions. Help students cut out the letters and glue them on the lines to spell each word. (**cat, cap, can**)
Day 5	Read the directions aloud and name the pictures together. Allow time for students to complete the first task. Then pronounce the words **cot** and **cop** and ask students to write them on the lines. Afterward, meet individually with students to discuss their results. Use their responses to plan further instruction and review.

Model the Skill

◆ Hand out the Day 1 activity page and some crayons.

◆ **Say:** *Let's pretend we're going camping. We can only bring things that begin with /k/. Can we bring corn or peppers? Color the one that starts with /k/.* Allow time for students to color the corn.

◆ **Ask:** *Can we bring a flashlight or a candle? Color the one that begins with /k/.* Allow time for students to color the candle.

◆ **Ask:** *Can we bring a camera or a TV? Color the one that begins with /k/.* Allow time for students to color the camera. Then ask them to draw one more item they can bring that begins with /k/. Invite them to share their drawings with the group.

◆ Point out objects you can see in the classroom that start with **/k/**. Write a few on chart paper and read the words aloud. Then invite students to add to the list.

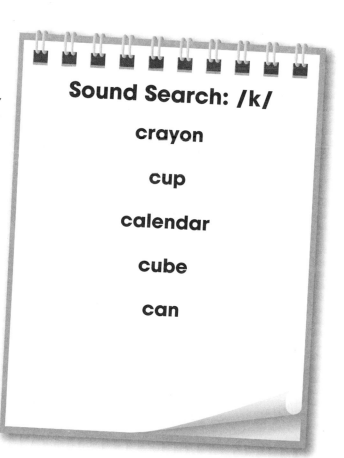

Sound Search: /k/

crayon

cup

calendar

cube

can

Name _____

Let's Go Camping

Color the things that start with /c/ like *can*.

Then draw something else that starts with /c/.

Unit 9 • Everyday Phonics Intervention Activities Grade 1 • ©2010 Newmark Learning, LLC

Callie's Farm

Welcome to Callie's farm. Say each picture aloud. Write *c* under the ones that begin with /k/.

Cart or Sack?

Cut out the pictures and name them. Glue the pictures that begin with /k/ in the cart. Glue the ones that begin with /s/ in the sack.

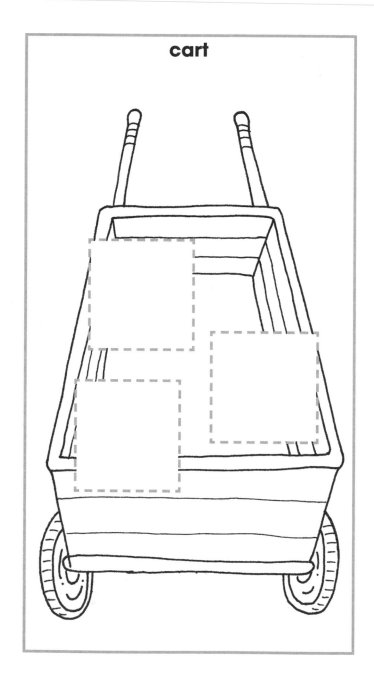

cart

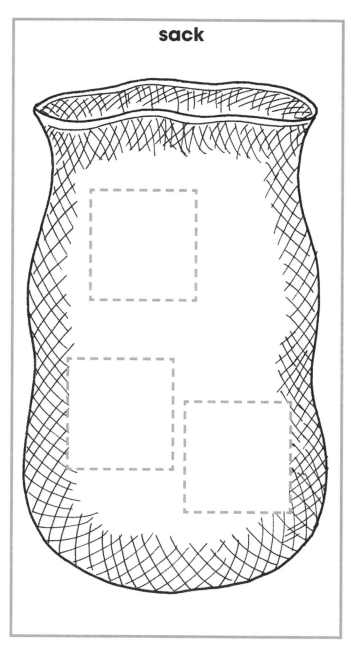

sack

Unit 9 • Everyday Phonics Intervention Activities Grade 1 • ©2010 Newmark Learning, LLC

Sound It Out

Say the picture word. Listen to the sounds at the beginning, middle, and end. Cut out the letters and glue them to make each word.

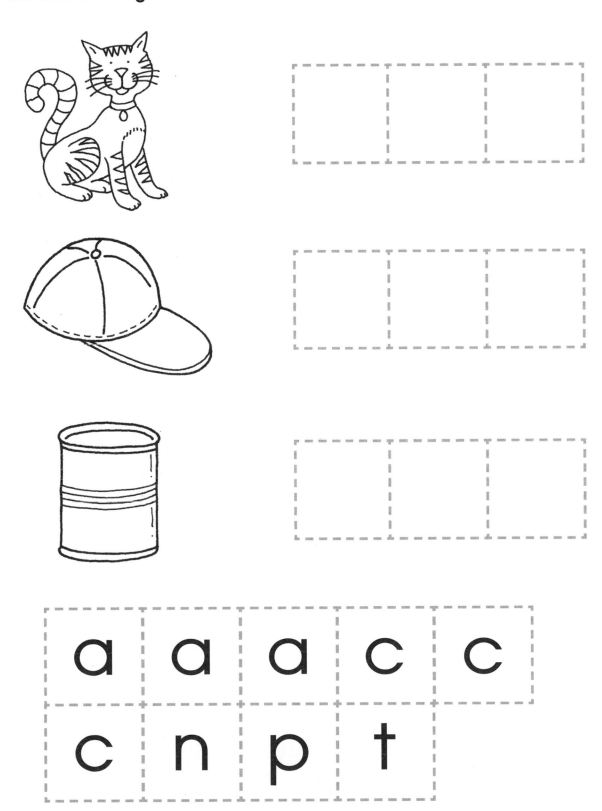

Assessment

Say the name of each picture. Write *c* if the word starts with */k/*.

_____   _____

_____   _____

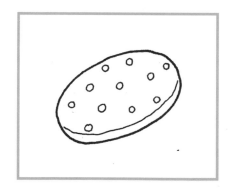

_____   _____

Listen to your teacher say each word. Write the words on the lines.

1. _____

2. _____

Overview Hh

Directions and Sample Answers for Activity Pages

Day 1	See "Model the Skill" below.
Day 2	Read the title and directions aloud. Invite students to name each picture. Then help students circle and write **h** under each picture that begins with **/h/**. (**hat, hose, house, hotdog, horse**)
Day 3	Read aloud the title and directions. Invite students to name each picture. Then help students glue the pictures that begin with **/h/** under the hat, **/k/** under the coat, and **/m/** under the mittens. (Hat: **hammer, hippo**. Coat: **carrot, candle**. Mittens: **mouse, map**.)
Day 4	Read aloud the title and directions. Help students cut out the letters and glue them on the lines to spell each word. (**hat, hit, ham**)
Day 5	Read the directions aloud and name the pictures together. Allow time for students to complete the first task. Then pronounce the words **hot** and **hip** and ask students to write them on the lines. Afterward, meet individually with students to discuss their results. Use their responses to plan further instruction and review.

Model the Skill

◆ Hand out the Day 1 activity page and some crayons.

◆ **Say:** *The human body has many parts that begin with* **/h/**. *Let's say the different parts aloud. If something begins with* **/h/**, *we'll color it in. Does* **hand** *begin with* **/h/**? Allow time for students to say the word with you and color it in.

◆ **Say:** *Listen to the word* **head**. *Do you hear* **/h/** *at the beginning?* Repeat the word **head**, stressing the **/h/** at the beginning. Invite students to say **head** aloud and then color it in. Repeat with the words **heel** and **heart**.

◆ **Ask:** *What is missing on this person's head? What sound do you hear at the beginning of* **hair**? **Hair** *starts with* **/h/**. Have students draw hair on the person.

◆ Name some animals that start with **/h/**. Write a few on chart paper and read the words aloud. Then invite students to add to the list.

Animal Sound Search: /h/

hog

horse

hippopotamus

hare

hamster

hedgehog

Human Body

Color the things that start with /h/ like *hat*. Then draw hair on the person.

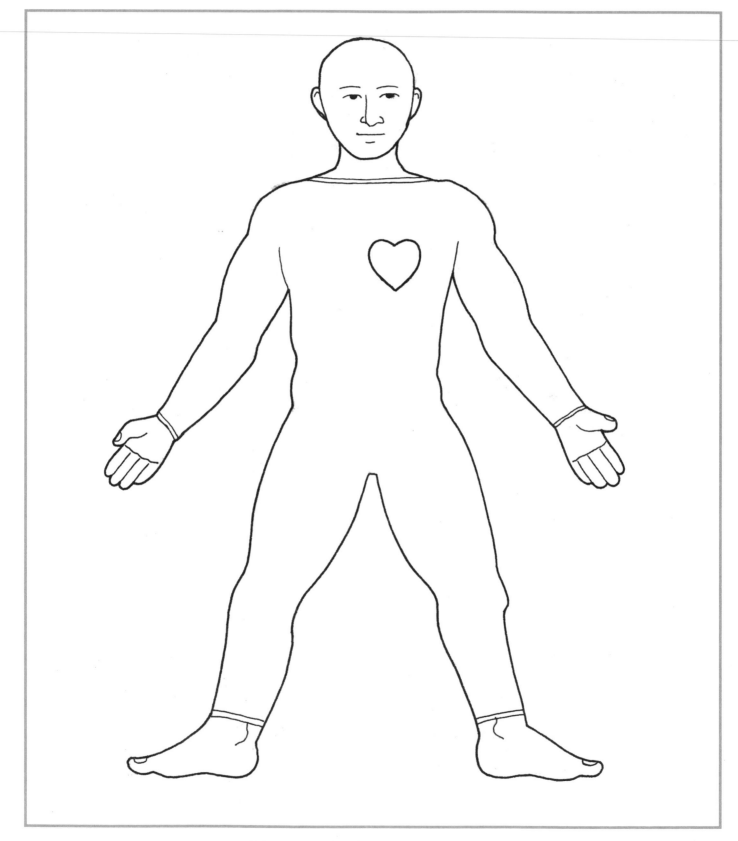

     Unit 10 • Everyday Phonics Intervention Activities Grade 1 • ©2010 Newmark Learning, LLC

Hop-Along Harry

Help Harry Hare hop over the hill.

Circle pictures that begins with /h/ and write an h under each one.

Hat, Coat, and Mittens

Cut out the pictures and name them. Glue the pictures that begin with /h/ under the hat. Glue the pictures that begin with /k/ under the coat. Glue the pictures that begin with /m/ under the mittens.

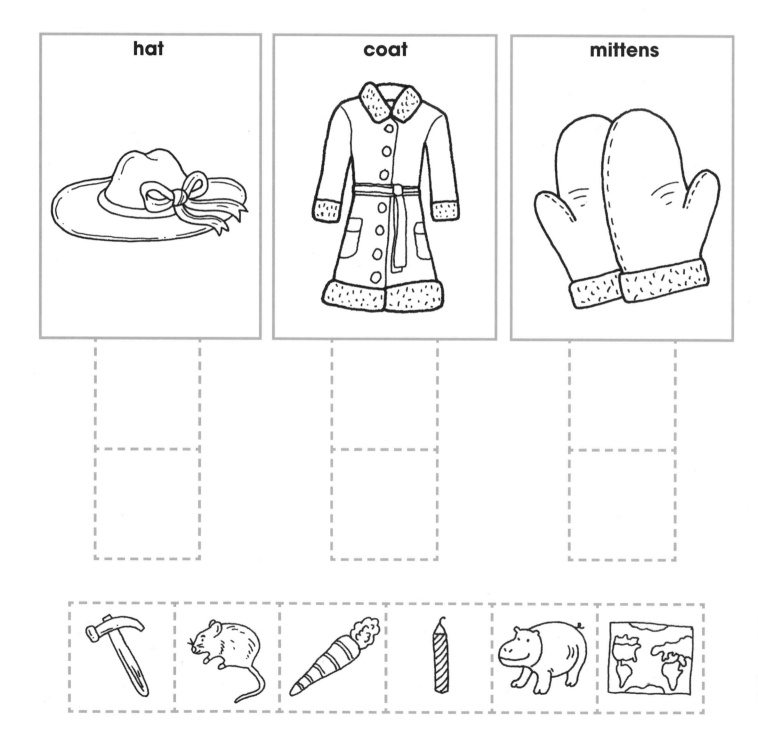

hat   coat   mittens

Sound It Out

Say the picture word. Listen to the sounds at the beginning, middle, and end.
Cut out the letters and glue them to spell each word.

Assessment

Say the name of each picture. Write **h** if the word starts with **/h/**.

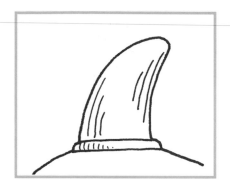

_____   _____

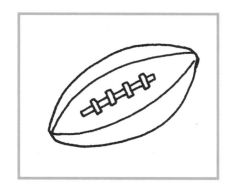

_____   _____

_____   _____

Listen to your teacher say each word. Write the words on the lines.

1. _____

2. _____

Overview   Bb

Directions and Sample Answers for Activity Pages

Day 1	See "Model the Skill" below.
Day 2	Read the title and directions aloud. Invite students to name each picture. Then help students write **b** under each picture that begins with **/b/**. (**blocks, blanket, bib, book, bear, ball**)
Day 3	Read aloud the title and directions. Invite students to name each picture. Then help students glue the pictures that begin with **/b/** under the bear and the pictures that end with **/b/** under the cub. (Bear: **bench, bed, bird**. Cub: **crib, tub, crab**.)
Day 4	Read aloud the title and directions. Help students cut out the letters and glue them on the lines to spell each word. (**bat, bib, cab**)
Day 5	Read the directions aloud and name the pictures together. Allow time for students to complete the first task. Then pronounce the words **bit** and **bat** and ask students to write them on the lines. Afterward, meet individually with students to discuss their results. Use their responses to plan further instruction and review.

Model the Skill

◆ Hand out the Day 1 activity page and some crayons.

◆ **Say:** *Let's pretend we are at the beach. When we see something that begins with /b/, let's color it blue. Does ball begin with /b/?* Allow time for students to say the word with you and color it blue. Repeat with **bucket** and **basket**. Then invite students to draw one more thing that begins with **/b/**.

◆ **Say:** *Now let's look for things that end with /b/ and color them yellow. Does crab end with /b/?* Allow time for students to say the word with you and color it yellow. Repeat with **tube**.

◆ Point out that many things we use every day start with **/b/**. Write a few on chart paper and read the words aloud. Then invite students to add to the list.

Sound Search: /b/

bike

ball

bat

bed

bus

brush

bench

Beach Day

Color the things that start with /b/ blue. Color the things that end with /b/ yellow.

Draw something else that starts with /b/.

Baby Bottle

Help the baby find her bottle. Write *b* under each picture that begins with /b/.

Name _____

Bear and Cub

Cut out the pictures. Glue the ones with the same beginning sound as *bear* under the big bear. Glue the pictures with the same ending sound as *cub* under the baby bear.

bear

cub

Unit 11 • Everyday Phonics Intervention Activities Grade 1 • ©2010 Newmark Learning, LLC

Sound It Out

Say the picture word. Listen to the sounds at the beginning, middle, and end.
Cut out the letters and glue them to spell the word.

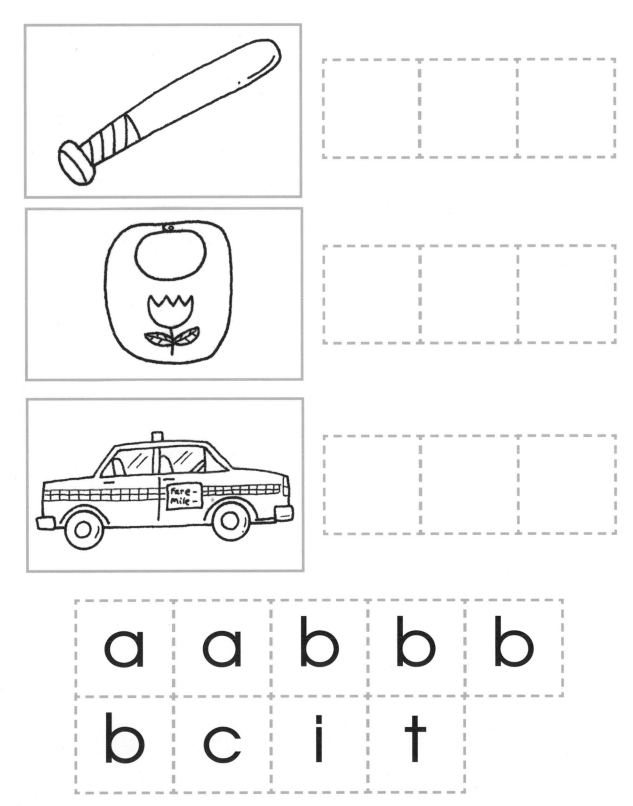

Assessment

Say the name of each picture. Write *b* if the word starts with */b/*.

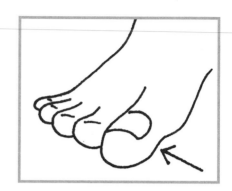

_____

_____

_____

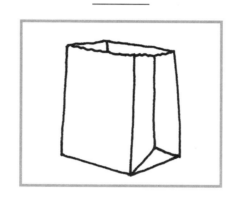

_____

_____

_____

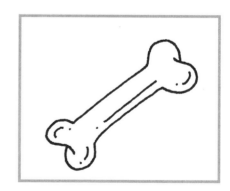

_____

_____

_____

Listen to your teacher say each word. Write the words on the lines.

1. _____

2. _____

Overview Short Uu

Directions and Sample Answers for Activity Pages

Day 1	See "Model the Skill" below.
Day 2	Read the title and directions aloud. Invite students to name each picture. Help students color the pictures that have the same middle sound as **fun** and **run**. (**cup, nut, bus, truck, rug, jug, skull**)
Day 3	Read aloud the title and directions. Invite students to name each picture. Then help students glue pictures with the same middle sound as **rug** on the rug. (**drum, gum, bug, duck**)
Day 4	Read aloud the title and directions. Help students sound out the words and write the missing letter to complete each one. (**bus, pot, nut, map, cub, bib**)
Day 5	Read the directions aloud and name the pictures together. Allow time for students to complete the first task. Then pronounce the words **hut** and **bun** and ask students to write them on the lines. Afterward, meet individually with students to discuss their results. Use their responses to plan further instruction and review.

Model the Skill

◆ Hand out the Day 1 activity page.

◆ **Say:** *Welcome to the great outdoors! Here you will find many things that have the /u/ sound in the middle. Do you hear /u/ in the middle of mud?* Allow time for students to say the word with you and mark **Yes**.

◆ **Ask:** *Does mouse have /u/ in the middle?* Point out that **mouse** has the letter **u** in it, but that it is not the same /u/ sound as in **mud**. Allow time for students to repeat the word with you and mark **No**.

◆ Repeat with the rest of the pictures. Then invite students to draw one more item with /u/ in the middle.

◆ Point out that many things from our daily lives have a /u/ sound. Write examples on chart paper. Then invite students to suggest other items.

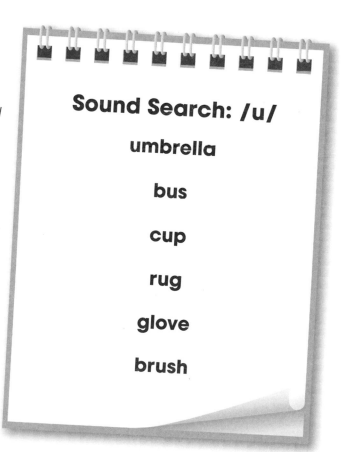

Sound Search: /u/

umbrella

bus

cup

rug

glove

brush

Outdoor Fun

Look at each picture. Does the picture have a /u/ sound like *mug*?

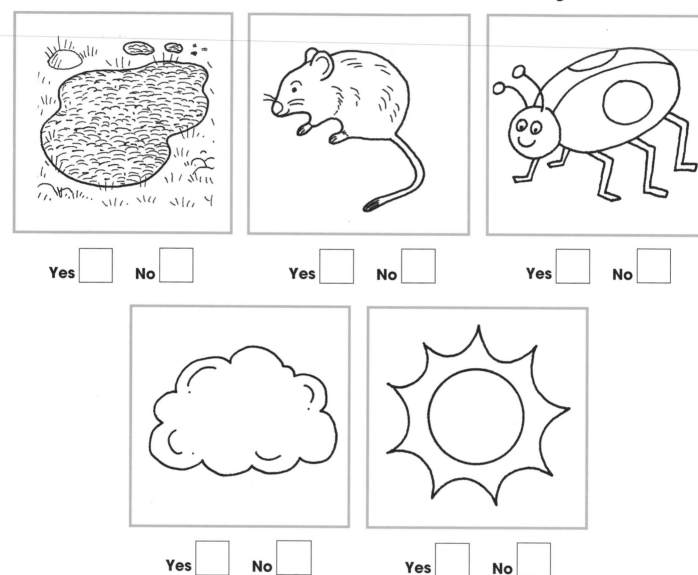

Yes ☐ No ☐   Yes ☐ No ☐   Yes ☐ No ☐

Yes ☐ No ☐   Yes ☐ No ☐

Fun Run

Color the pictures that have the same middle sound as *fun* and *run*.

Snug As a Bug on a Rug

Cut out and name each picture.

Glue the ones with the same middle sound as *rug* on the rug.

rug

Unit 12 • Everyday Phonics Intervention Activities Grade 1 • ©2010 Newmark Learning, LLC

Sound It Out

Name the picture. Write the letter that belongs in the middle.

Assessment

Say the name of each picture. Write **u** if the word has **/u/** in it.

_____

_____

_____

_____

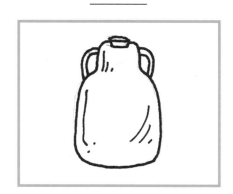

_____

_____

_____

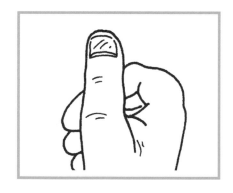

_____

_____

Listen to your teacher say each word. Write the words on the lines.

1. _____

2. _____

Unit 12 • Everyday Phonics Intervention Activities Grade 1 • ©2010 Newmark Learning, LLC

Overview Rr

Directions and Sample Answers for Activity Pages

Day 1	See "Model the Skill" below.
Day 2	Read aloud the title and directions. Invite students to name each picture. Then help students write X on each picture that begins with **/r/** and O on each picture that ends with **/r/**. (X: **rain, rake, rat, ring, rose**. O: **hammer, ladder, guitar, car**.)
Day 3	Read aloud the title and directions. Invite students to name each picture. Then help students glue the pictures that begin with **/r/** under the ring and the pictures that end with **/r/** under the finger. (Ring: **rocket, raindrop, rabbit**. Finger: **spider, chair, door**.)
Day 4	Read aloud the title and directions. Invite students to name each picture. Then help them read aloud each word and match the words to the pictures.
Day 5	Read the directions aloud and name the pictures together. Allow time for students to complete the first task. Then pronounce the words **rip** and **bar** and ask students to write them on the lines. Afterward, meet individually with students to discuss their results. Use their responses to plan further instruction and review.

Model the Skill

◆ Hand out the Day 1 activity page.

◆ **Say:** *Imagine we are taking a ride down the river. When we see something that begins with /r/, let's draw a circle around it. Does* **rock** *begin with /r/?* Allow time for students to say the word with you and circle it. Repeat with **rainbow** and **rowboat**. Then invite students to draw one more thing that begins with **/r/**. Tell them it can be something silly that they might not really see on a river.

◆ **Say:** *Now let's look for things that end with /r/ and draw a square around them. Does* **oar** *end with /r/?* Allow time for students to say the word with you and draw a square around it. Repeat with **skier** and **pear**. Then invite students to draw one more thing that ends with **/r/**.

◆ Point out that our homes are full of items that begin with **/r/**. Write a few on chart paper and read the words aloud. Then invite students to add to the list.

Sound Search: /r/

room

roof

robe

rug

refrigerator

radio

River Ride

Draw a circle around the things that start with /r/ like *rug*.

Draw a square around the things that end with /r/ like *car*.

Draw something else that has an /r/.

Tic-Tac-Toe

Write an X on each picture that begins with the same sound as *rabbit*. Write an O on each picture that ends with the same sound as *bear*. Which animal wins?

R Sort

Cut out the pictures. Glue the pictures that begin with /r/ under the ring.
Glue the pictures that end with /r/ under the finger.

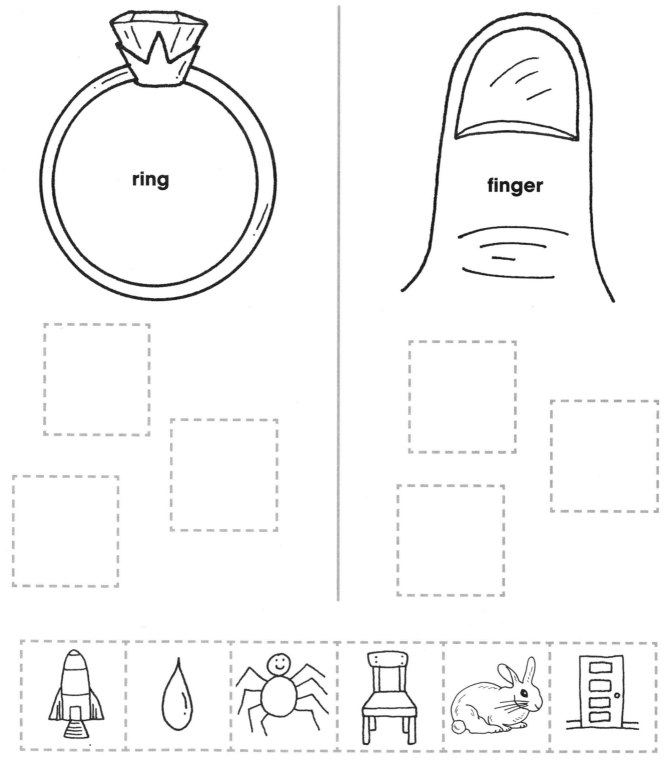

ring

finger

Make a Match

Name the pictures and listen to the sounds. Then read the words.
Draw a line from each word to its picture.

car

rat

run

ram

Assessment

Say the name of each picture. Write *r* if the word starts with /r/.

_____   _____   _____

_____   _____   _____

 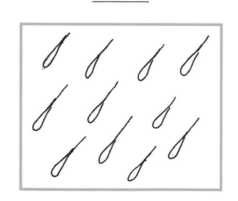 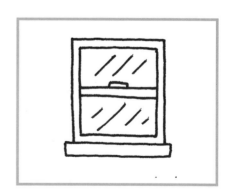

_____   _____   _____

Listen to your teacher say each word. Write the words on the lines.

1. _____

2. _____

   Unit 13 • Everyday Phonics Intervention Activities Grade 1 • ©2010 Newmark Learning, LLC

Overview   Short Ee

Directions and Sample Answers for Activity Pages

Day 1	See "Model the Skill" below.
Day 2	Read the title and directions aloud. Invite students to name each picture. Help students circle the picture and write the letter **e** if it has the same middle sound as **Nell**. (**bell, desk, shell, tent**)
Day 3	Read aloud the title and directions. Invite students to name each picture. Then help students glue pictures with the same middle sound as **Ned** in Ned's net. Help them glue pictures with the same beginning sound as **Ed** in Ed's net. (Ned: **vest, belt, hen**. Ed: **egg, elbow, elephant**.)
Day 4	Read aloud the title and directions. Invite students to name each picture. Then help them read aloud each word and match the words to the pictures.
Day 5	Read the directions aloud and name the pictures together. Allow time for students to complete the first task. Then pronounce the words **ten** and **red** and ask students to write them on the lines. Afterward, meet individually with students to discuss their results. Use their responses to plan further instruction and review.

Model the Skill

◆ Hand out the Day 1 activity page and a red crayon.

◆ **Say:** *Ted likes the color red. He also likes the number ten. In fact, Ted only likes things that have /e/ in the middle. Does Ted like his bed or his chair? Color the one with /e/ in the middle.* Allow time for students to color the bed.

◆ **Ask:** *Does Ted like his bike or his sled? Color the picture that has the /e/ sound in it.* Allow time for students to color the sled.

◆ **Ask:** *Does Ted prefer to use a crayon or a pen? Color the one that has /e/ in the middle.* Allow time for students to color the pen. Then ask them to draw one more thing with /e/ in it. Invite them to share their drawings with the group.

◆ Name actions people do that have the /e/ sound in the middle of the word. Write a few on chart paper and read the words aloud. Then invite students to add to the list.

Sound Search: /e/

step

help

tell

yell

guess

get

bend

check

Ted

Color the things that have an /e/ sound like *Ted*.
Then draw something else that has an /e/ sound.

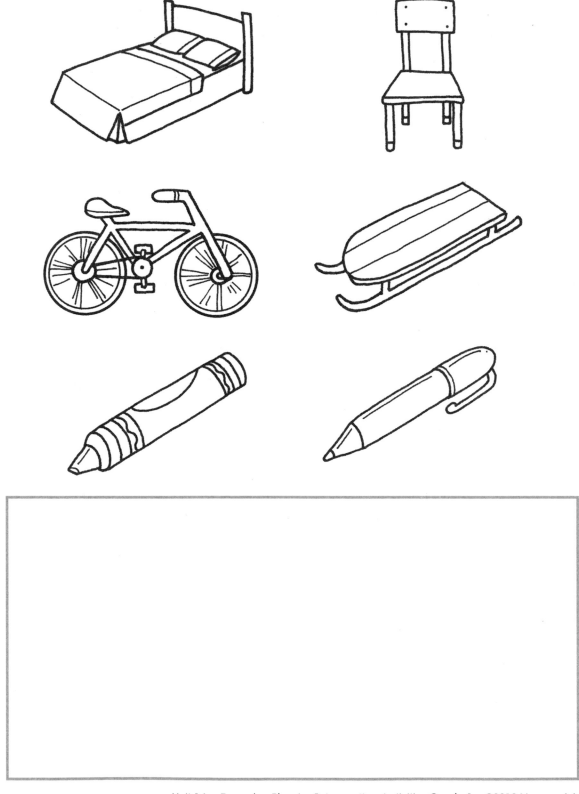

Unit 14 • Everyday Phonics Intervention Activities Grade 1 • ©2010 Newmark Learning, LLC

Name _____

Nell Sells

Nell sells things that have the same middle sound as her name.

Circle things that Nell can sell in her store.

Then write the letter *e* on the line below.

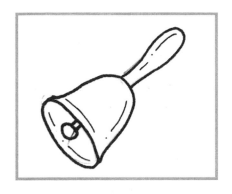

_____

_____

_____

_____

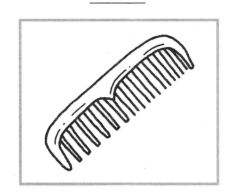

_____

_____

_____

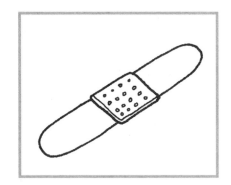

_____

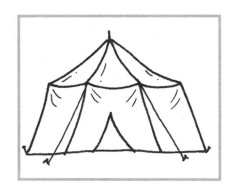

_____

Ned and Ed

Cut out and name each picture.

Glue the pictures with the same middle sound as *Ned* in Ned's net.

Glue the pictures that begin with the same sound as *Ed* in Ed's net.

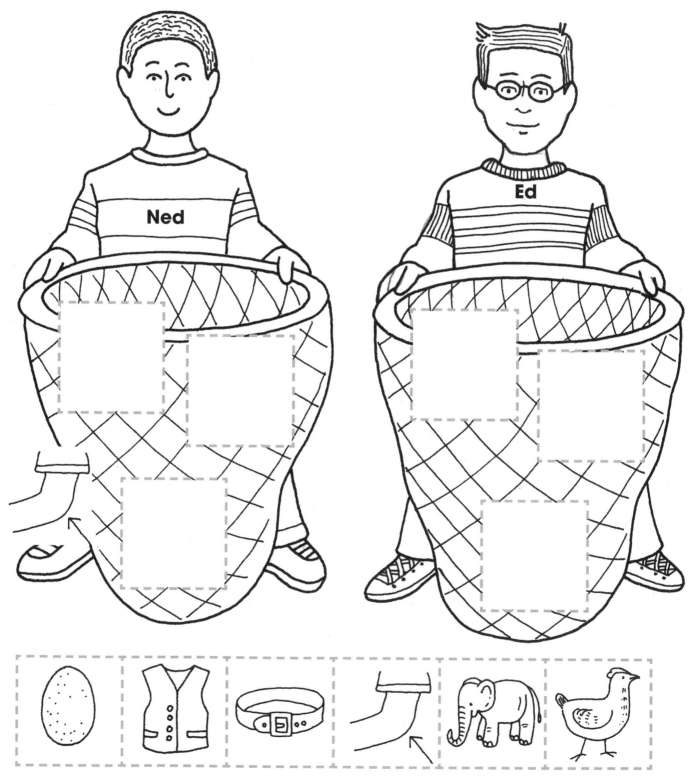

Make a Match

Name the pictures and listen to the sounds. Then read the words.
Draw a line from each word to its picture.

hen

pets

bed

men

Assessment

Say the name of each picture. Write *e* if the word has /e/ in it.

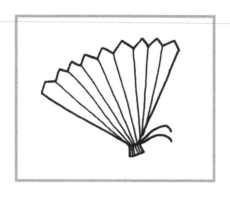

_____

_____

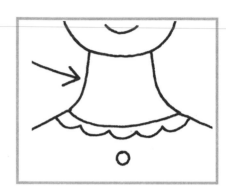

_____

_____

_____

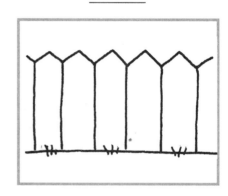

_____

_____

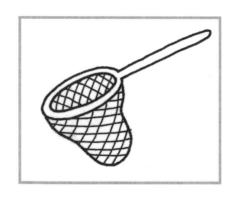

_____

_____

Listen to your teacher say each word. Write the words on the lines.

1. _____

2. _____

Overview Gg

Directions and Sample Answers for Activity Pages

Day 1	See "Model the Skill" below.
Day 2	Read aloud the title and directions. Invite students to name each picture. Then help students color the logs with pictures of things that begin with **/g/**. (**goat, grapes, gift, girl**)
Day 3	Read aloud the title and directions. Invite students to name each picture. Then help students glue the pictures that end with **/g/** under the bag and the pictures that begin with **/g/** under the garbage can. (Bag: **wig**, **pig**, **bug**. Garbage can: **globe**, **gate**, **grass**.)
Day 4	Read aloud the title and directions. Invite students to name each picture. Then help them read aloud the phrases and match the phrases to the pictures.
Day 5	Read the directions aloud and name the pictures together. Allow time for students to complete the first task. Then pronounce the words **sag** and **gap** and ask students to write them on the lines. Afterward, meet individually with students to discuss their results. Use their responses to plan further instruction and review.

Model the Skill

◆ Hand out the Day 1 activity page.

◆ **Say:** *Gary is having a garage sale, but he only plans to sell things that start with the same sound as his name. Let's circle the items in his garage that Gary can sell. Does **guitar** begin with **/g/**?* Allow time for students to say the word with you and circle it. Repeat with **golf clubs** and **gum**. Then invite students to draw one more thing that begins with **/g/**.

◆ **Say:** *Now let's look for things that end with **/g/** and draw a square around them. Does **rug** end with **/g/**?* Allow time for students to say the word with you and draw a square around it. Repeat with **jug** and **flag**. Then invite students to draw one more thing that ends with **/g/**.

◆ Say a student's name in the class, or the school, that has **/g/** in it. Write the name on chart paper. Then invite students to suggest other names.

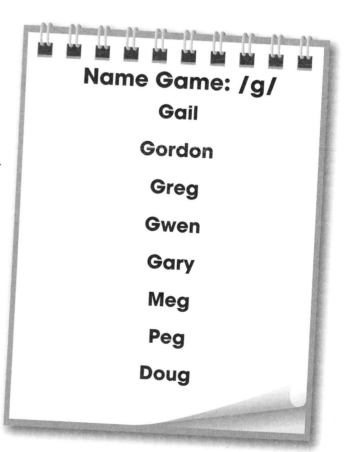

Name Game: /g/

Gail

Gordon

Greg

Gwen

Gary

Meg

Peg

Doug

Gary's Tag Sale

Draw a circle around the things that start with /g/ like *give*.

Draw a square around the things that end with /g/ like *tag*.

Draw something that begins with /g/.

Draw something that ends with /g/.

Log Leap

Help Frog leap across the pond.

Color the logs that show things that begin with /g/.

Name _____

Bag It or Can It

Cut out and name each picture. Glue the pictures that end with /g/ in the bag.
Glue the pictures that begin with /g/ in the garbage can.

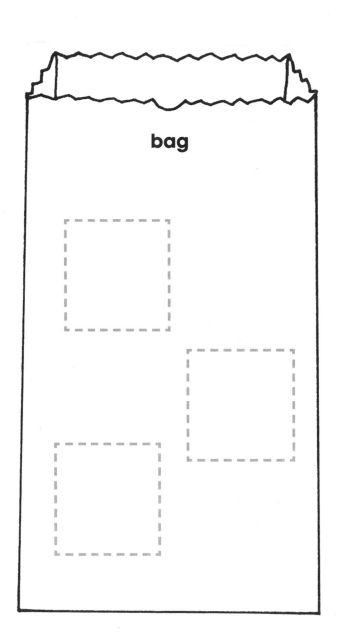

bag

garbage can

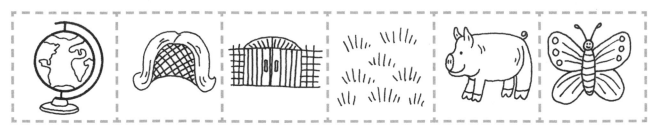

Make a Match

Name the pictures. Then read the words.
Draw a line to match the words and pictures.

bug   sat

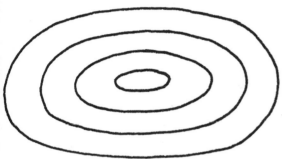

hug   pig

Meg   runs

big   rug

Name _____

Assessment

Say the name of each picture. Write *g* if the word starts or ends with /g/.

_____

_____

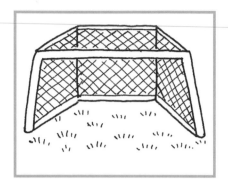

_____

_____

_____

_____

_____

_____

Listen to your teacher say each word. Write the words on the lines.

1. _____

2. _____

 Unit 15 • Everyday Phonics Intervention Activities Grade 1 • ©2010 Newmark Learning, LLC

Overview Dd

Directions and Sample Answers for Activity Pages

Day 1	See "Model the Skill" below.
Day 2	Read aloud the title and directions. Invite students to name each picture. Then help students color the pictures of toys that begin with **/d/**. (**doll, duck, drum, dog**)
Day 3	Read aloud the title and directions. Invite students to name each picture. Then help students glue the pictures that begin with **/d/** under the dog and the pictures that end with **/d/** under the bed. (Dog: **dot, dinosaur, duck, door**. Bed: **cloud, sled**.)
Day 4	Read aloud the title and directions. Invite students to name each picture. Then help them read aloud the phrases and match the phrases to the pictures.
Day 5	Read the directions aloud and name the pictures together. Allow time for students to complete the first task. Then pronounce the words **bad** and **dim** and ask students to write them on the lines. Afterward, meet individually with students to discuss their results. Use their responses to plan further instruction and review.

Model the Skill

◆ Hand out the Day 1 activity page.

◆ **Say:** *Donna is having a dance party. Everyone must dress up as something that begins with **/d/** or bring something that begins with **/d/**. Can I dress up as a firefighter or a doctor?* Allow time for students to color the doctor.

◆ **Ask:** *Can I bring doughnuts or cookies? Color the treat that begins with **/d/**.* Allow time for students to color the doughnuts.

◆ **Ask:** *Can I bring dance shoes or snow boots? Color the ones that begin with **/d/**.* Allow time for students to color the dance shoes. Then ask them to draw one more item for the party that begins with **/d/**. Invite them to share their drawings with the group.

◆ Point out objects you can see in the classroom that start or end with **/d/**. Write a few on chart paper and read the words aloud. Then invite students to add to the list.

Sound Search: /d/

desk

door

dice

pad

word

kid

Name _____

Donna's Dance Party

Color the things that start with a **/d/** sound like *door*.

Then draw something else that begins with a **/d/** sound.

Unit 16 • Everyday Phonics Intervention Activities Grade 1 • ©2010 Newmark Learning, LLC

D Is for . . .

Color the toys that begin with /d/.

 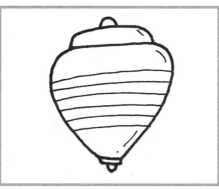 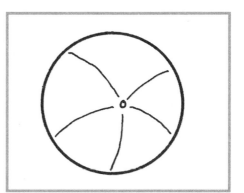

  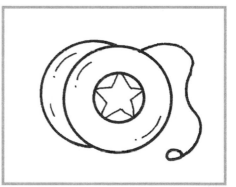

D Sort

Cut out the pictures. Glue the pictures that begin with /d/ under the dog.
Glue the pictures that end with /d/ under the bed.

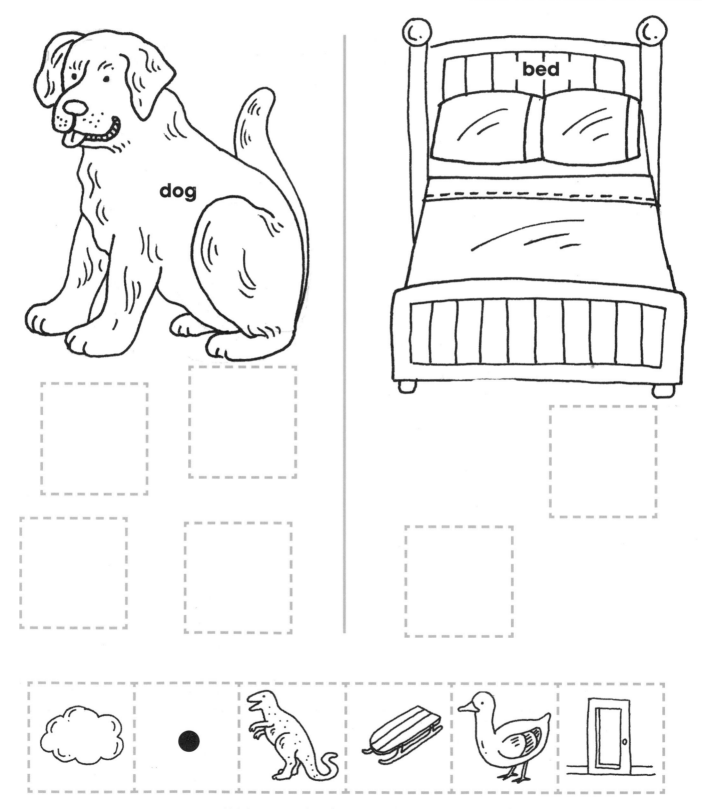

dog

bed

Unit 16 • Everyday Phonics Intervention Activities Grade 1 • ©2010 Newmark Learning, LLC

Make a Match

Name the pictures. Then read the words.
Draw a line to match the pictures and words.

sad dad

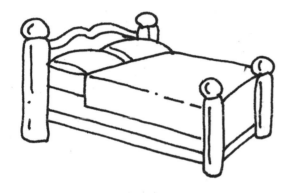

Peg dug

mad cat

big bed

Assessment

Say the name of each picture. Write *d* if the word starts with /d/.

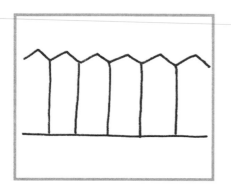

_____   _____   _____

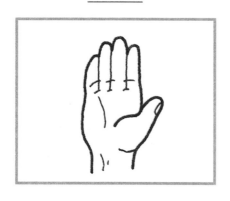

_____   _____   _____

_____   _____   _____

Listen to your teacher say each word. Write the words on the lines.

1. _____

2. _____

    Unit 16 • Everyday Phonics Intervention Activities Grade 1 • ©2010 Newmark Learning, LLC

Overview Ww

Directions and Sample Answers for Activity Pages

Day 1	See "Model the Skill" below.
Day 2	Read the title and directions aloud. Invite students to name each picture. Then help students write **w** under each picture that begins with **/w/**. (**wand, wagon, wink, window, wheel**)
Day 3	Read aloud the title and directions. Invite students to name each picture. Then help students glue the pictures that begin with **/w/** in the well. (**watch, worm, wolf**)
Day 4	Read aloud the title and directions. Help students cut out the letters and glue them on the lines to spell each word. (**wig, win, wet**)
Day 5	Read the directions aloud and name the pictures together. Allow time for students to complete the first task. Then pronounce the words **win** and **wet** and ask students to write them on the lines. Afterward, meet individually with students to discuss their results. Use their responses to plan further instruction and review.

Model the Skill

◆ Hand out the Day 1 activity page and crayons.

◆ **Say:** *Welcome to Wendy's backyard. There are many things here that begin with the same sound as* **welcome** *and* **Wendy**. *When we see something that begins with* **/w/**, *let's color it in. Does* **watermelon** *begin with* **/w/**? *Allow time for students to say the word with you and color it in. Repeat with* **wagon**, **worm**, **water**, *and* **window**. *Then invite students to draw one more thing that begins with* **/w/**.

◆ Point out the many things we use every day that begin with **/w/**. Write a few on chart paper and read the words aloud. Then invite students to add to the list.

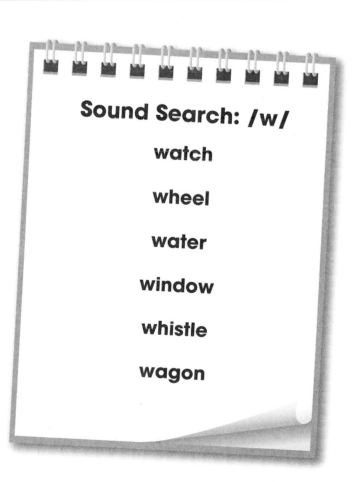

Sound Search: /w/

watch

wheel

water

window

whistle

wagon

Wendy Welcomes You

Color the things that start with a /w/ sound like *Wendy*.
Then draw something else that has a /w/ sound.

Willy Worm

Help Willy Worm dig his way home.
Write _w_ under each picture that begins with /w/.

Into the Well

Cut out and color the pictures that begin with the same sound as *well*.
Then glue those words in the well.

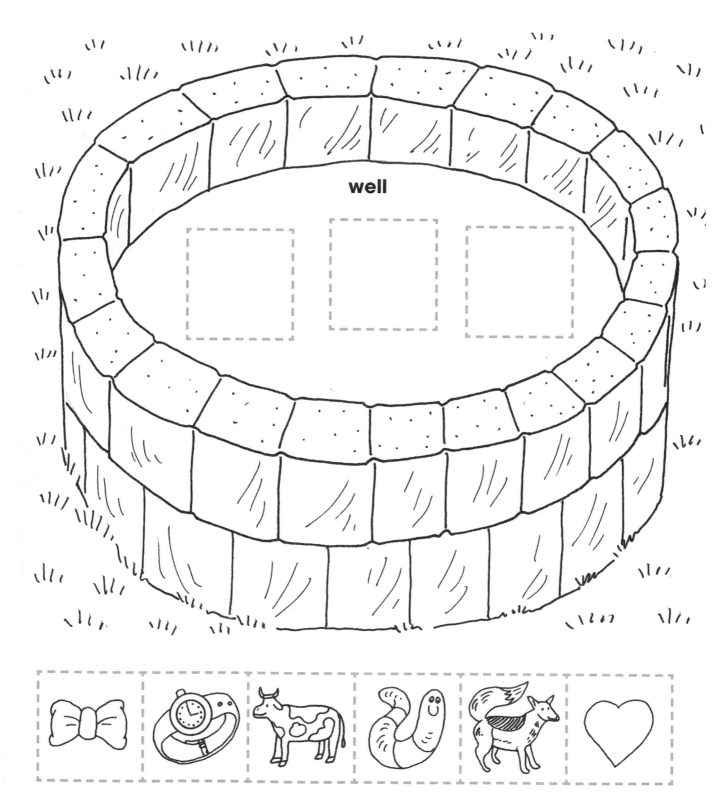

well

Sound It Out

Say the picture word. Listen to the sounds at the beginning, middle, and end.
Cut out the letters and glue them to spell the word.

Assessment

Say the name of each picture. Write *w* if the word starts with /w/.

 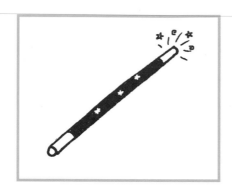 

_____ _____ _____

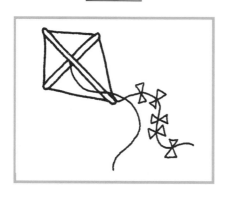  

_____ _____ _____

_____ _____ _____

Listen to your teacher say each word. Write the words on the lines.

1. _____

2. _____

Overview   Ll

Directions and Sample Answers for Activity Pages

Day 1	See "Model the Skill" below.
Day 2	Read the title and directions aloud. Invite students to name each picture. Then help students circle each picture that begins with **/l/**. (**lightbulb, lion, leg, leaf, lemon**)
Day 3	Read aloud the title and directions. Invite students to name each picture. Then help students glue the pictures that begin with **/l/** under the lion and the pictures that end with **/l/** under the camel. (Lion: **ladder, log, leaf**. Camel: **bowl, wheel, nail**.)
Day 4	Read aloud the title and directions. Invite students to name each picture. Then help them read aloud each word and match the words to the pictures.
Day 5	Read the directions aloud and name the pictures together. Allow time for students to complete the first task. Then pronounce the words **let** and **pal** and ask students to write them on the lines. Afterward, meet individually with students to discuss their results. Use their responses to plan further instruction and review.

Model the Skill

◆ Hand out the Day 1 activity page.

◆ **Say:** *Lucy collects things that begin and end with /l/. First, let's find things in her room that begin with /l/ and circle them. Does lamp begin with /l/?* Allow time for students to say the word with you and then circle it. Repeat with **lollipop** and **lion**. Then invite students to draw one more thing that begins with **/l/**.

◆ **Say:** *Now let's look for things that end with /l/ and draw a square around them. Does bell end with /l/?* Allow time for students to say the word with you and draw a square around it. Repeat with **doll** and **pencil**. Then invite students to draw one more thing that ends with **/l/**.

◆ Say a student's name in the class, or the school, that has the **/l/** sound in it. Write the name on chart paper. Then invite students to suggest other names.

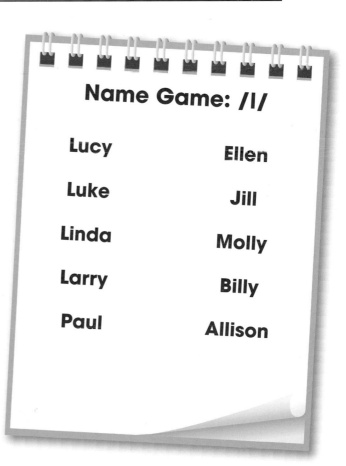

Name Game: /l/

Lucy	Ellen
Luke	Jill
Linda	Molly
Larry	Billy
Paul	Allison

What Lucy Loves

Draw a circle around the things that start with /l/ like *lap*.

Draw a square around the things that end with /l/ like *pal*.

Draw something that begins with /l/.

Draw something that ends with /l/.

Lizzy Gets Lemons

Help Lizzy reach the lemons. Circle the things that begin with /l/.

Lion or Camel

Cut out the pictures. Glue the pictures with the same beginning sound as *lion* under the lion. Glue the pictures with the same ending sound as *camel* under the camel.

lion	camel

Unit 18 • Everyday Phonics Intervention Activities Grade 1 • ©2010 Newmark Learning, LLC

Name _____

Make a Match

Name the pictures and listen to the sounds. Then read the words.
Draw a line from each picture to its word.

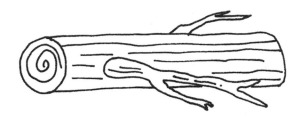

lips

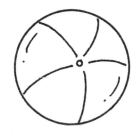

doll

log

ball

Name _____

Assessment

Say the name of each picture. Write *l* if the word starts with /*l*/.

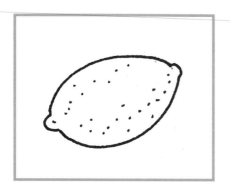

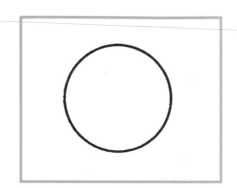

_____

_____

_____

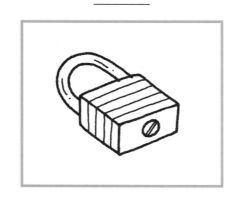

_____

_____

_____

_____

_____

_____

Listen to your teacher say each word. Write the words on the lines.

1. _____

2. _____

Overview   Jj

Directions and Sample Answers for Activity Pages

Day 1	See "Model the Skill" below.
Day 2	Read the title and directions aloud. Invite students to name each picture. Then help students circle each picture that begins with **/j/**. (**jellybeans, jacks, juice, jeans**)
Day 3	Read aloud the title and directions. Invite students to name each picture. Then help students glue the pictures that begin with **/j/** in Jacob's jar and the pictures that begin with **/a/** in Abby's jar. (Jacob: **jam, jump rope, jeep**. Abby: **apple, alligator, ant**.)
Day 4	Read aloud the title and directions. Help students cut out the letters and glue them on the lines to spell each word. (**jog, jet, jam**)
Day 5	Read the directions aloud and name the pictures together. Allow time for students to complete the first task. Then pronounce the words **jet** and **jog** and ask students to write them on the lines. Afterward, meet individually with students to discuss their results. Use their responses to plan further instruction and review.

Model the Skill

◆ Hand out the Day 1 activity page and crayons.

◆ **Say:** *Welcome to the jungle! Let's pretend we are going on a hunt for things that start with /j/. When we find them, let's color them in. Does jaguar begin with /j/?* Allow time for students to say the word with you and then color it in.

◆ **Say:** *What is the boy holding that begins with /j/? That's right! He's holding a jug. Let's color it in.* Continue this type of questioning with **jacket** and **jeep**. Allow time for students to say the words and color them in. Then invite students to draw one more thing that begins with **/j/**. Tell them it can be something silly that they may not really see in a jungle.

◆ Name actions people do that begin with **/j/**. Write a few on chart paper and read the words aloud. Then invite students to add to the list.

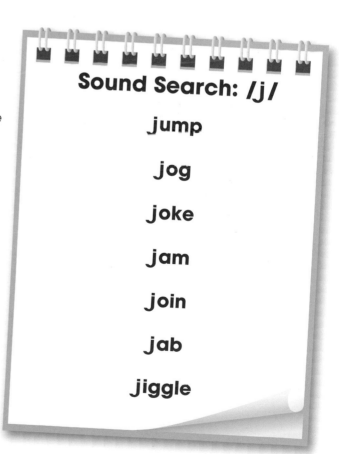

Sound Search: /j/

jump

jog

joke

jam

join

jab

jiggle

Jungle Fun

Color the things that start with a /j/ sound like *job*.

Then draw something else that has a /j/ sound.

Jill Jumps

Jill jumps on things that begin with /j/. Circle the pictures Jill can jump on.

Name _____

Jacob or Abby

Help Jacob and Abby sort their things. Cut out the pictures.

Glue the pictures with the same beginning sound as *Jacob* in Jacob's jar.

Glue the pictures with the same beginning sound as *Abby* in Abby's jar.

Jacob **Abby**

Name _____

Sound It Out

Say the picture word. Listen to the sounds at the beginning, middle, and end.
Cut out the letters and glue them to spell each word.

Assessment

Say the name of each picture. Write *j* if the word starts with /*j*/.

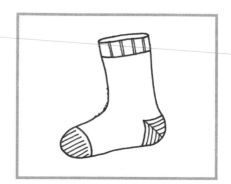

_____   _____   _____

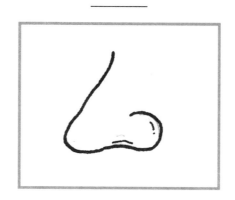

_____   _____   _____

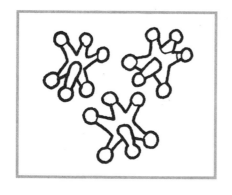

_____   _____   _____

Listen to your teacher say each word. Write the words on the lines.

1. _____

2. _____

Overview   Kk

Directions and Sample Answers for Activity Pages

Day 1	See "Model the Skill" below.
Day 2	Read aloud the title and directions. Invite students to name each picture. Then help students write **k** under pictures that begin with **/k/**. (**kite, key, koala, king, kitten**)
Day 3	Read aloud the title and directions. Invite students to name each picture. Then help students glue the pictures that begin with **/k/** in the cart and the pictures that end with **/k/** in the sack. (Cart: **cow, kite, computer**. Sack: **book, lock, sock**.)
Day 4	Read aloud the title and directions. Invite students to name each picture. Then help them read aloud the phrases and match the phrases to the pictures.
Day 5	Read the directions aloud and name the pictures together. Allow time for students to complete the first task. Then pronounce the words **kit** and **kid** and ask students to write them on the lines. Afterward, meet individually with students to discuss their results. Use their responses to plan further instruction and review.

Model the Skill

◆ Hand out the Day 1 activity page and crayons.

◆ **Say:** *Today is **K** day at school. All the kids are to bring in something that begins with **/k/**. Can they bring a puppy or a kitten? Color the one that begins with **/k/**.* Allow time for students to color the kitten.

◆ **Ask:** *Can they bring a kite or a yo-yo? Color the toy that begins with **/k/**.* Allow time for students to color the kite.

◆ **Ask:** *Can they bring a key or a lock? Color the one that begins with **/k/**.* Allow time for students to color the key. Then ask them to draw one object that begins with **/k/**. Invite them to share their drawings with the group.

◆ Say a student's name in the class, or the school, that has the **/k/** sound in it. Write the name on chart paper. Then invite students to suggest other names.

Name Game: /k/

Katie	Chuck
Kyle	Frank
Keith	Karen
Kurt	Keesha
Mark	Kelsey

K Day

Color the things that start with a /k/ sound like *kiss*.

Then draw something else that has a /k/ sound.

Kangaroo Hop

Kandy Kangaroo only hops on things that begin with /k/.
Write **k** under the pictures that begin with /k/.

Pack It Up

Name the pictures and cut them out.

Glue the ones with the same beginning sound as *cart* in the cart.

Glue the pictures with the same ending sound as *sack* in the sack.

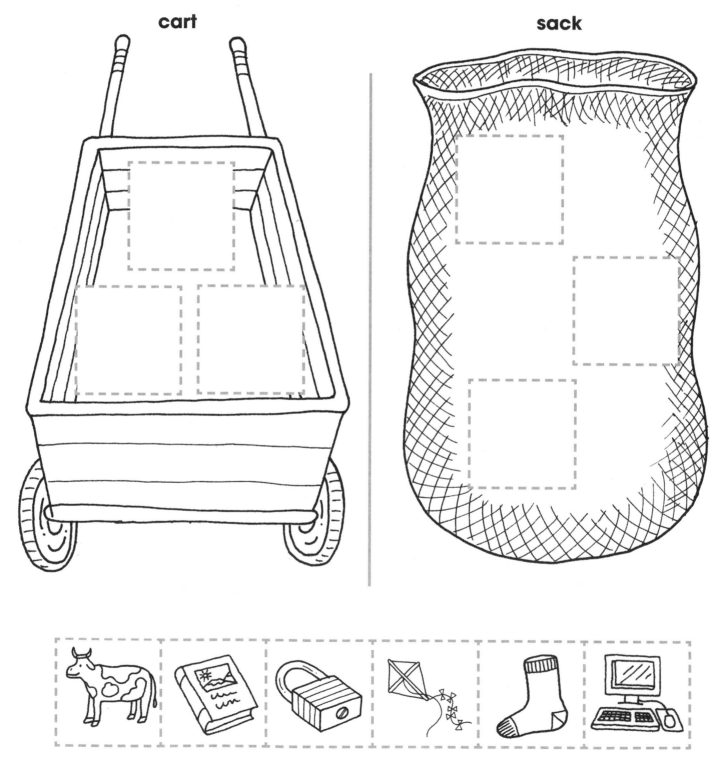

cart

sack

Unit 20 • Everyday Phonics Intervention Activities Grade 1 • ©2010 Newmark Learning, LLC

Make a Match

Name the pictures. Then read the words.
Draw a line to match the pictures and words.

mad kid

run Kim

big kiss

Assessment

Say the name of each picture. Write **k** if the word starts with /k/.

_____

_____

_____

_____

_____

_____

_____

_____

_____

Listen to your teacher say each word. Write the words on the lines.

1. _____

2. _____

Overview   Yy

Directions and Sample Answers for Activity Pages

Day 1	See "Model the Skill" below.
Day 2	Read the title and directions aloud. Invite students to name each action. Help students circle the picture and write the letter **y** if it begins with **/y/**. (**yawn, yoga, yell, yank, yodel**)
Day 3	Read aloud the title and directions. Invite students to name each picture. Then help students glue pictures that begin with **/y/** in the basket. (**yarn, yolk, yo-yo**)
Day 4	Read aloud the title and directions. Invite students to name each picture. Then help them read aloud the phrases and match the phrases to the pictures.
Day 5	Read the directions aloud and name the pictures together. Allow time for students to complete the first task. Then pronounce the words **yes** and **bay** and ask students to write them on the lines. Afterward, meet individually with students to discuss their results. Use their responses to plan further instruction and review.

Model the Skill

◆ Hand out the Day 1 activity page and yellow crayons.

◆ **Say:** *This is Yolanda's yard. There are many things here that begin with the same sound as* **yard**. *When we find things that begin with* **/y/**, *let's color them yellow. Does* **yo-yo** *begin with* **/y/**? Allow time for students to say the word with you and color it yellow.

◆ Repeat with **yak**, **yoga**, and **yogurt**. Then invite students to draw one more thing that begins with **/y/**. Tell them it can be something silly that they might not really see in a yard.

◆ Point out some objects and actions that begin with **/y/**. Write a few on chart paper and read the words aloud. Then invite students to add to the list.

Sound Search: /y/

you	**year**
yard	**yell**
yawn	**yarn**
yellow	**yoga**
yesterday	**yogurt**
yank	

Y Search

Color the things that start with a /y/ sound like *you*.

Then draw something else that has a /y/ sound.

Y on the Move

Circle each action that begins with /y/ and write *y* under the picture.

_____

_____

_____

_____

_____

_____

_____

_____

_____

Y Sort

Cut out and name each picture. Glue the ones that begin with /y/ in the basket.

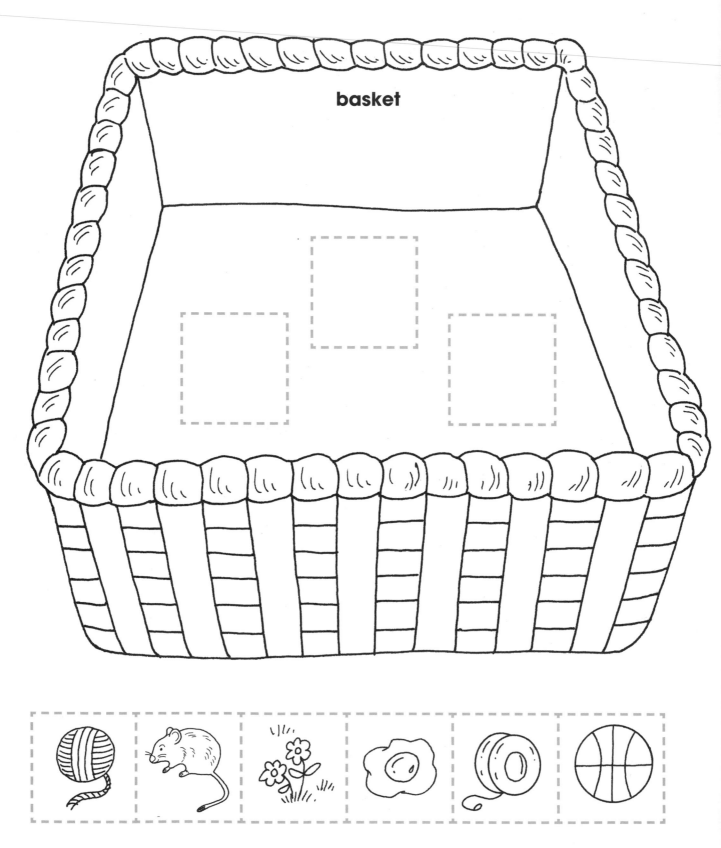

basket

Unit 21 • Everyday Phonics Intervention Activities Grade 1 • ©2010 Newmark Learning, LLC

Make a Match

Name the pictures. Then read the words.
Draw a line to match the pictures and words.

kid   yell

big   yam

yak   nap

Assessment

Say the name of each picture. Write **y** if the word begins with **/y/**.

_____

_____

_____

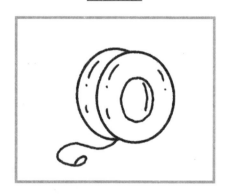

_____

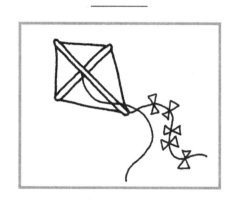

_____

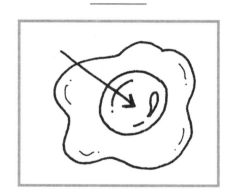

_____

_____

_____

_____

Listen to your teacher say each word. Write the words on the lines.

1. _____

2. _____

Unit 21 • Everyday Phonics Intervention Activities Grade 1 • ©2010 Newmark Learning, LLC

Overview Vv

Directions and Sample Answers for Activity Pages

Day 1	See "Model the Skill" below.
Day 2	Read aloud the title and directions. Invite students to name each picture. Then help students write X on each picture that begins with **/v/** and O on each picture that ends with **/v/**. (X: **vase, vine, volcano, vampire**. O: **wave, glove, five, dove, stove**.)
Day 3	Read aloud the title and directions. Invite students to name each picture. Then help students glue the pictures that begin with **/v/** in the vase and pictures that end with **/v/** in the cave. (Vase: **vacuum cleaner, vet, volcano, vine**. Cave: **glove, hive**.)
Day 4	Read aloud the title and directions. Help students cut out the letters and glue them on the lines to spell each word. (**van, vet, vase**)
Day 5	Read the directions aloud and name the pictures together. Allow time for students to complete the first task. Then pronounce the words **vet** and **van** and ask students to write them on the lines. Afterward, meet individually with students to discuss their results. Use their responses to plan further instruction and review.

Model the Skill

◆ Hand out the Day 1 activity page and some crayons.

◆ **Say:** *Pretend you are going on vacation, but you can only pack things that begin with the same sound as* **vacation**. *Can you pack a vest or a jacket? Color the clothing that starts with* **/v/**. Allow time for students to color the vest.

◆ **Ask:** *Can you pack vegetables or fruit? Color the food that begins with* **/v/**. Allow time for students to color the vegetables.

◆ **Ask:** *Can you pack a flute or a violin? Color the instrument that begins with* **/v/**. Allow time for students to color the violin. Then ask them to draw one more item they can bring that begins with **/v/**. Invite them to share their drawings with the group.

◆ Point out objects you can see in the classroom that have a **/v/** in them. Write a few on chart paper and read the words aloud. Then invite students to add to the list.

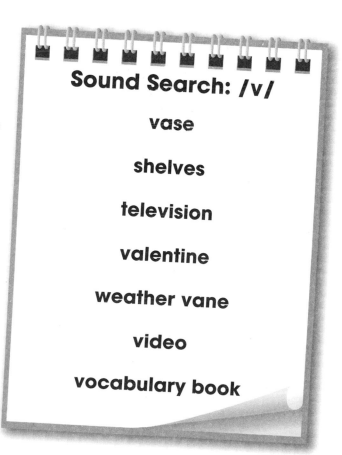

Sound Search: /v/

vase

shelves

television

valentine

weather vane

video

vocabulary book

Name _____

Vacation

Color the things that have a /v/ sound like *van*.

Then draw something else that begins with a /v/ sound.

Tic-Tac-Toe

Write an **X** on each picture that begins with the same sound as *Vin*.

Write an **O** on each picture that ends with the same sound as *Liv*.

Which friend wins?

V Sort

Cut out and name each picture. Glue the pictures that begin with /v/ in the vase.
Glue the pictures that end with /v/ in the cave.

vase   cave

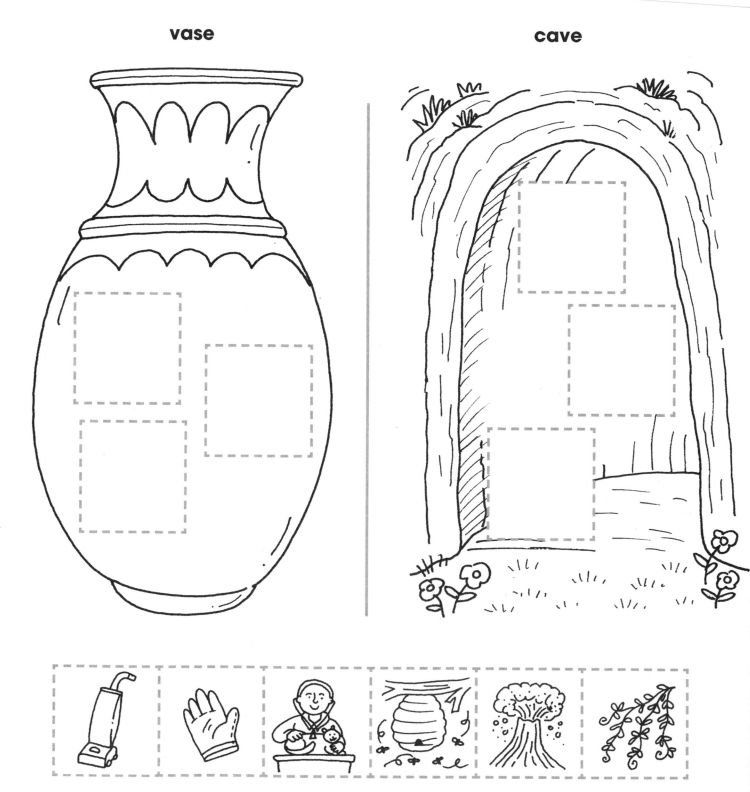

Unit 22 • Everyday Phonics Intervention Activities Grade 1 • ©2010 Newmark Learning, LLC

Sound It Out

Say the picture word. Listen to the sounds at the beginning, middle, and end.
Cut out the letters and glue them to spell the word.

Assessment

Say the name of each picture. Write *v* if the word starts with /v/.

 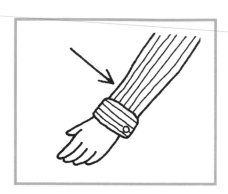 

_____   _____   _____

_____   _____   _____

_____   _____

Listen to your teacher say each word. Write the words on the lines.

1. _____

2. _____

Unit 22 • Everyday Phonics Intervention Activities Grade 1 • ©2010 Newmark Learning, LLC

Overview   Qq

Directions and Sample Answers for Activity Pages

Day 1	See "Model the Skill" below.
Day 2	Read aloud the title and directions. Invite students to name each picture. Then help students draw a line from each item that begins with **/kw/** to the quacking duck. (**question mark, queen, quail, quilt, quart**)
Day 3	Read aloud the title and directions. Invite students to name each picture. Then help students glue the pictures that begin with **/kw/** onto the quilt. (**queen, question mark, quill, quart**)
Day 4	Read aloud the title and directions. Invite students to name each picture. Then help them read aloud the phrases and match the phrases to the pictures.
Day 5	Read the directions aloud and name the pictures together. Allow time for students to complete the first task. Then pronounce the words **quit** and **quip** and ask students to write them on the lines. Afterward, meet individually with students to discuss their results. Use their responses to plan further instruction and review.

Model the Skill

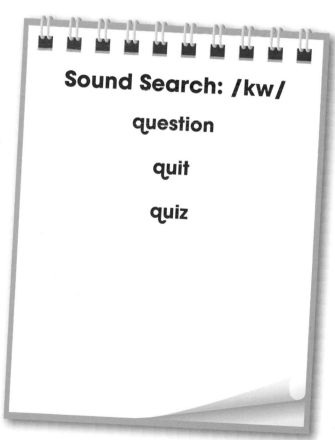

◆ Hand out the Day 1 activity page and some crayons.

◆ **Say:** *The Queen of Q Castle insists that everything inside begin with the same sound as* **queen**. *Does the queen cover her bed with a blanket or a quilt? Color the one that begins with* **/kw/**. Allow time for students to color the quilt.

◆ **Ask:** *What type of coins does the queen carry: quarters or dimes? Color the coin that begins with* **/kw/**. Allow time for students to color the quarter.

◆ **Ask:** *Do you think the queen writes with a pencil or a quill? Color the one that begins with* **/kw/**.

◆ Point out things we do that begin with **/kw/**. Write a few on chart paper and read the words aloud. Challenge students to find more actions that begin with **/kw/** to add to the list.

Sound Search: /kw/

question

quit

quiz

Queen's Castle

Color the things that have a /kw/ sound like *quit*. Then draw something else that has a /kw/ sound.

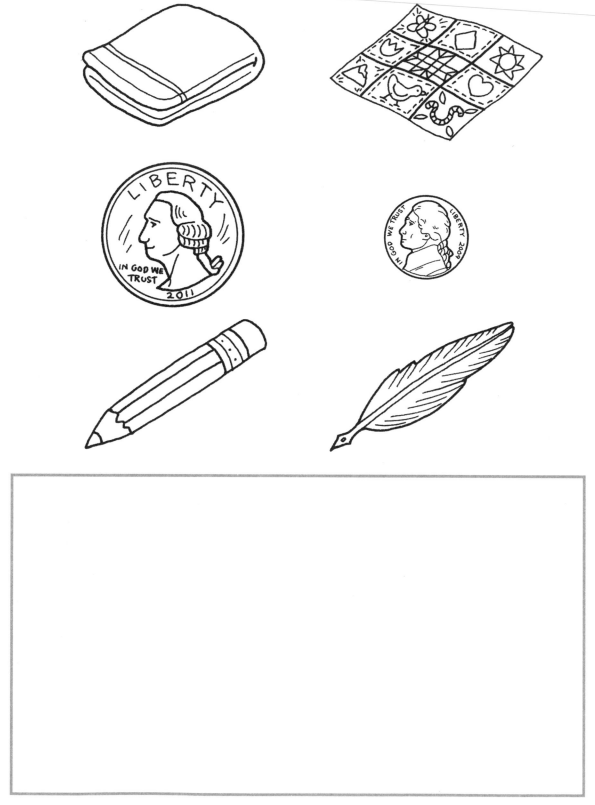

Quack Quack

Draw a line from Quack the Duck to items that begin with the same sound as *quack.*

Make a Quilt

Cut out and name each picture.

Glue the pictures that begin with /kw/ onto the quilt.

Unit 23 • Everyday Phonics Intervention Activities Grade 1 • ©2010 Newmark Learning, LLC

Make a Match

Name the pictures. Then read the words.
Draw a line to match the pictures and words.

mad queen

duck quack

quick cat

Assessment

Say the name of each picture. Write *q* if the word starts with */kw/*.

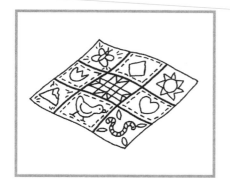

_____

_____

_____

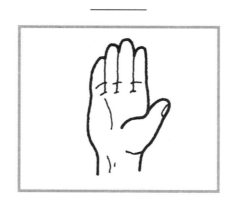

_____

_____

_____

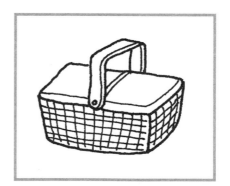

_____

_____

Listen to your teacher say each word. Write the words on the lines.

1. _____

2. _____

Overview   Xx

Directions and Sample Answers for Activity Pages

Day 1	See "Model the Skill" below.
Day 2	Read aloud the title and directions. Invite students to name each picture. Then help students draw a line from each item with a **/ks/** sound to the X. (**taxi, fox, saxophone, mix, X-ray, sixty**)
Day 3	Read aloud the title and directions. Invite students to name each picture. Then help students glue the pictures that have the same end sound as **mix** in the mixing bowl. (**ox, six, box, ax**)
Day 4	Read aloud the title and directions. Help students cut out the letters and glue them on the lines to spell each word. (**six, box, ax**)
Day 5	Read the directions aloud and name the pictures together. Allow time for students to complete the first task. Then pronounce the words **fix** and **tax** and ask students to write them on the lines. Afterward, meet individually with students to discuss their results. Use their responses to plan further instruction and review.

Model the Skill

◆ Hand out the Day 1 activity page.

◆ **Say:** *Let's pack in our box things that end with the same sound as* **box**. *Do you hear* **/ks/** *at the end of* **fox**? Allow time for students to say the word with you and mark **Yes**.

◆ **Ask:** *Does* **xylophone** *end like* **box**? Point out that **xylophone** has the letter **x** in it, but it does not make the **/ks/** sound and is not at the end of the word. Allow time for students to repeat the word with you and mark **No**.

◆ Repeat with the rest of the pictures. Then invite students to draw one more thing they could pack that ends with the same sound as **box**.

◆ Point out some things and actions that have an **/ks/** sound in them. Write examples on chart paper. Then invite students to suggest other items.

Sound Search: /ks/

fix

mix

exit

fax

taxi

Name _____

X in the Box

Look at each picture. Does it have an */ks/* sound like *box*?

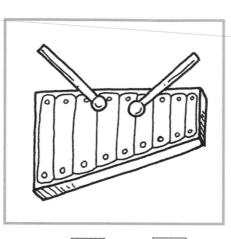

Yes ☐ No ☐   Yes ☐ No ☐   Yes ☐ No ☐

Yes ☐ No ☐   Yes ☐ No ☐

Draw something else that has an */ks/* sound.

X Marks the Spot

Draw a line from the X to items that have an */ks/* sound in them.

In the Mix

Cut out and name each picture.

Glue the pictures that have the same end sound as *mix* in the mixing bowl.

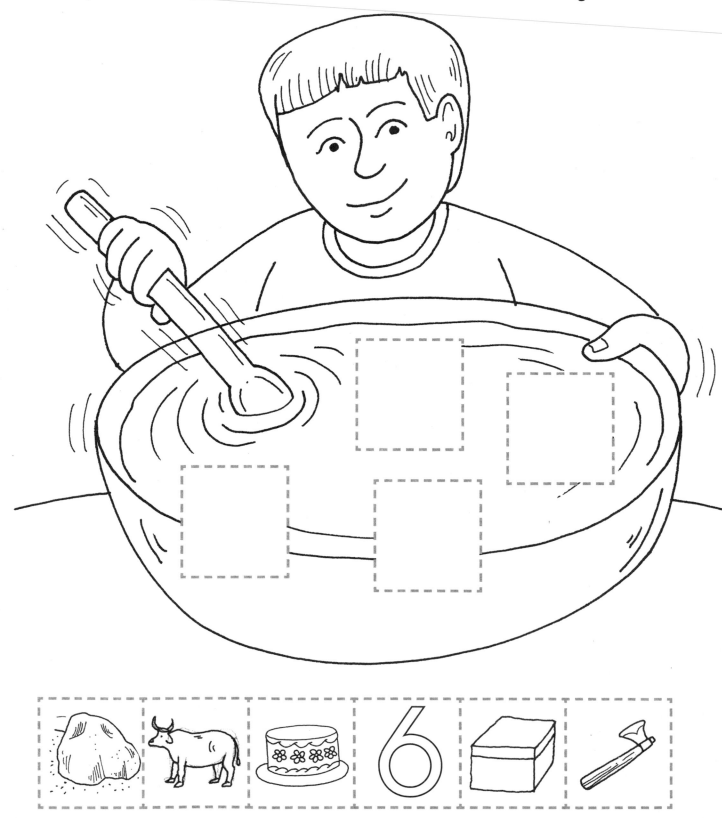

Unit 24 · Everyday Phonics Intervention Activities Grade 1 · ©2010 Newmark Learning, LLC

Sound It Out

Say the picture word. Listen to the sounds at the beginning, middle, and end.
Cut out the letters and glue them to spell the word.

Assessment

Say the name of each picture. Write *x* if you hear the */ks/* sound.

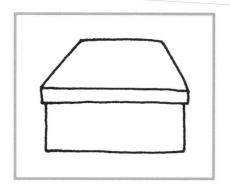

_____

_____

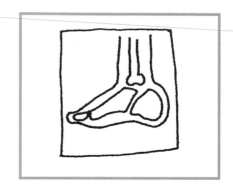

_____

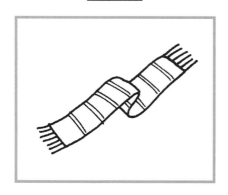

_____

_____

_____

_____

_____

_____

Listen to your teacher say each word. Write the words on the lines.

1. _____

2. _____

Overview Zz

Directions and Sample Answers for Activity Pages

Day 1	See "Model the Skill" below.
Day 2	Read the title and directions aloud. Invite students to name each picture. Then help students write **z** under each picture that has a **/z/** in it. (**zero, sneeze, zipper, razor**)
Day 3	Read aloud the title and directions. Invite students to name each picture. Then help students glue the pictures that begin with **/z/** under Zed and the pictures that end with **/z/** under Liz. (Zed: **zipper, zebra, zero**. Liz: **doze, maze, prize**.)
Day 4	Read aloud the title and directions. Invite students to name each picture. Then help them read aloud the phrases and match the phrases to the pictures.
Day 5	Read aloud the directions and name the pictures together. Allow time for students to complete the first task. Then pronounce the words **zip** and **zap** and ask students to write them on the lines. Afterward, meet individually with students to discuss their results. Use their responses to plan further instruction and review.

Model the Skill

◆ Hand out the Day 1 activity page and crayons.

◆ **Say:** *This is Zack. Zack loves things that begin with the same sound as his name. Let's find and color all the things in this picture that begin with **/z/**. Does **zebra** begin with **/z/**?* Allow time for students to say the word with you and color it in.

◆ Repeat with **zoo** and **zipper**. Then invite students to draw one more thing that begins with **/z/**.

◆ Point out some actions that have a **/z/** sound in them. Write examples on chart paper. Then invite students to suggest other items.

Sound Search: /z/

zip

zap

zoom

doze

daze

freeze

sneeze

squeeze

quiz

Zack Loves Z

Color the things that have a /z/ sound like *zip*. Then draw something that has a /z/.

Unit 25 • Everyday Phonics Intervention Activities Grade 1 • ©2010 Newmark Learning, LLC

Zebra's Maze

Help Zebra find his way to the zoo. Write *z* under each picture that has a */z/* sound in it.

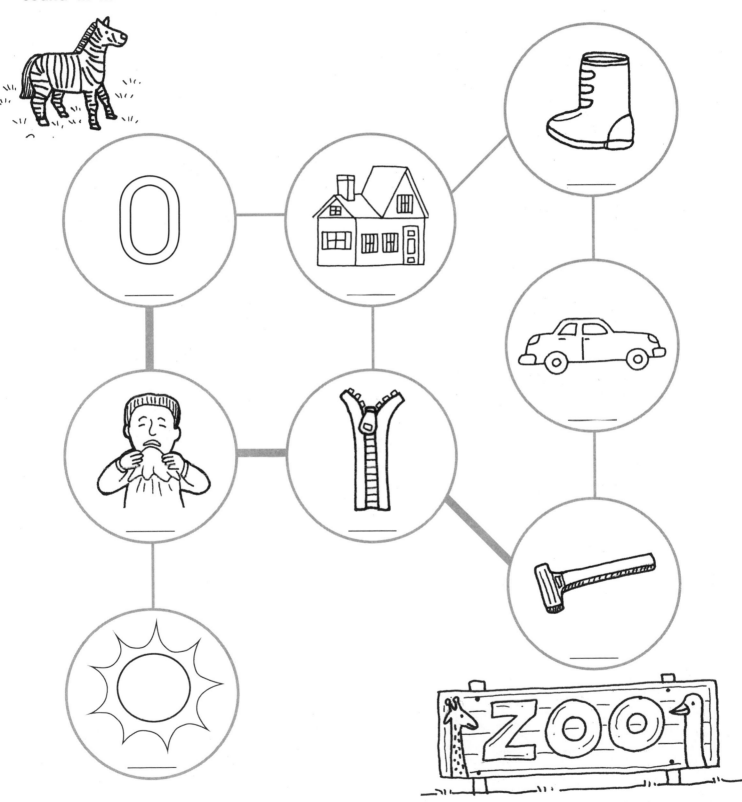

Name _____

Zed or Liz

Cut out the pictures. Glue the ones with the same beginning sound as *Zed* under Zed. Glue the pictures with the same ending sound as *Liz* under Liz.

Zed

Liz

Unit 25 • Everyday Phonics Intervention Activities Grade 1 • ©2010 Newmark Learning, LLC

Make a Match

Name the pictures. Then read the words. Draw a line to match the pictures and words.

Liz zips

bee buzz

mad dogs

Assessment

Say the name of each picture. Write *z* if you hear the /z/ sound.

_____

_____

_____

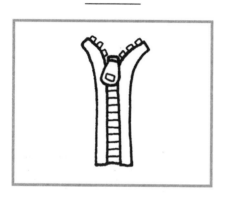

_____

_____

_____

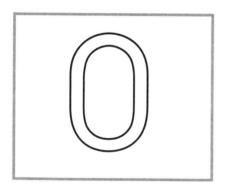

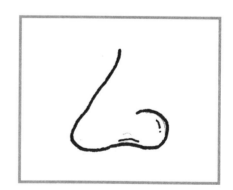

_____

_____

_____

Listen to your teacher say each word. Write the words on the lines.

1. _____

2. _____

Unit 25 • *Everyday Phonics Intervention Activities* Grade 1 • ©2010 Newmark Learning, LLC

Notes

Notes

Everyday Phonics Intervention Activities Grade 1 • ©2010 Newmark Learning, LLC

Notes

Notes